AF471009

NEW
GIRL
ORDER

NEW GIRL ORDER

Iain McKell

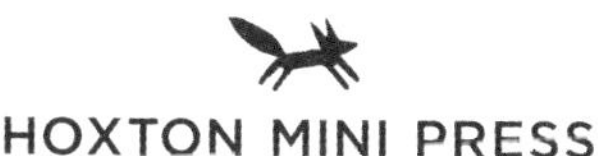

HOXTON MINI PRESS

IAIN MCKELL

Known for documenting counter-cultures in the UK and around the world, Iain is a British fine art-documentary, fashion and portrait photographer who lives in London. He enjoys working on long-term personal projects and his practice is invested in the human psyche of individuals and communities. Iain began taking photographs in his hometown Weymouth, Dorset – during the mid to late 70s while studying graphic design at Exeter College of Art and Design. These images would later become the series 'Private Reality: A Diary of a Teenage Boy'.

Iain has photographed various sub-societies including New York's Guardian Angels, the mod/skinhead revival in the 80s from London to Southend and horse-drawn New Age travellers in the West Country (1986–2010) which became a book, *The New Gypsies*. Over the years he has made portraits of icons like Madonna and Kate Moss, directed commercials and pop videos and worked on commission for *The Sunday Times, Vogue Italia, L'Uomo Vogue* and *i-D*. Iain's work has been exhibited in numerous galleries including The Photographers' Gallery (London, 1985) and the Turner Contemporary (Margate, 2019) and this is his fifth photography book. He continues to shoot editorial fashion, portraits and advertisements while working on long-term documentary projects. Visit www.iainmckell.com to see more of Iain's work.

HOXTON MINI PRESS

Hoxton Mini Press is a tiny, award-winning independent publisher based in East London. Our goal is to make photography books that are beautiful but also accessible: neither snooty nor aloof but easy to pick up whilst still feeling special. We started out by making books just about East London, working with local photographers and writers. We now make books about topics all over the world but we are still grounded in London and inspired by the local, urban stories of neighbourhood life.

As the world goes online and digital photographs become easier to take, share (and then throw away) we believe that books, and the stories within them, should be cherished and kept on for generations. To see more of our books please visit www.hoxtonminipress.com or follow us on social media @hoxtonminipress.

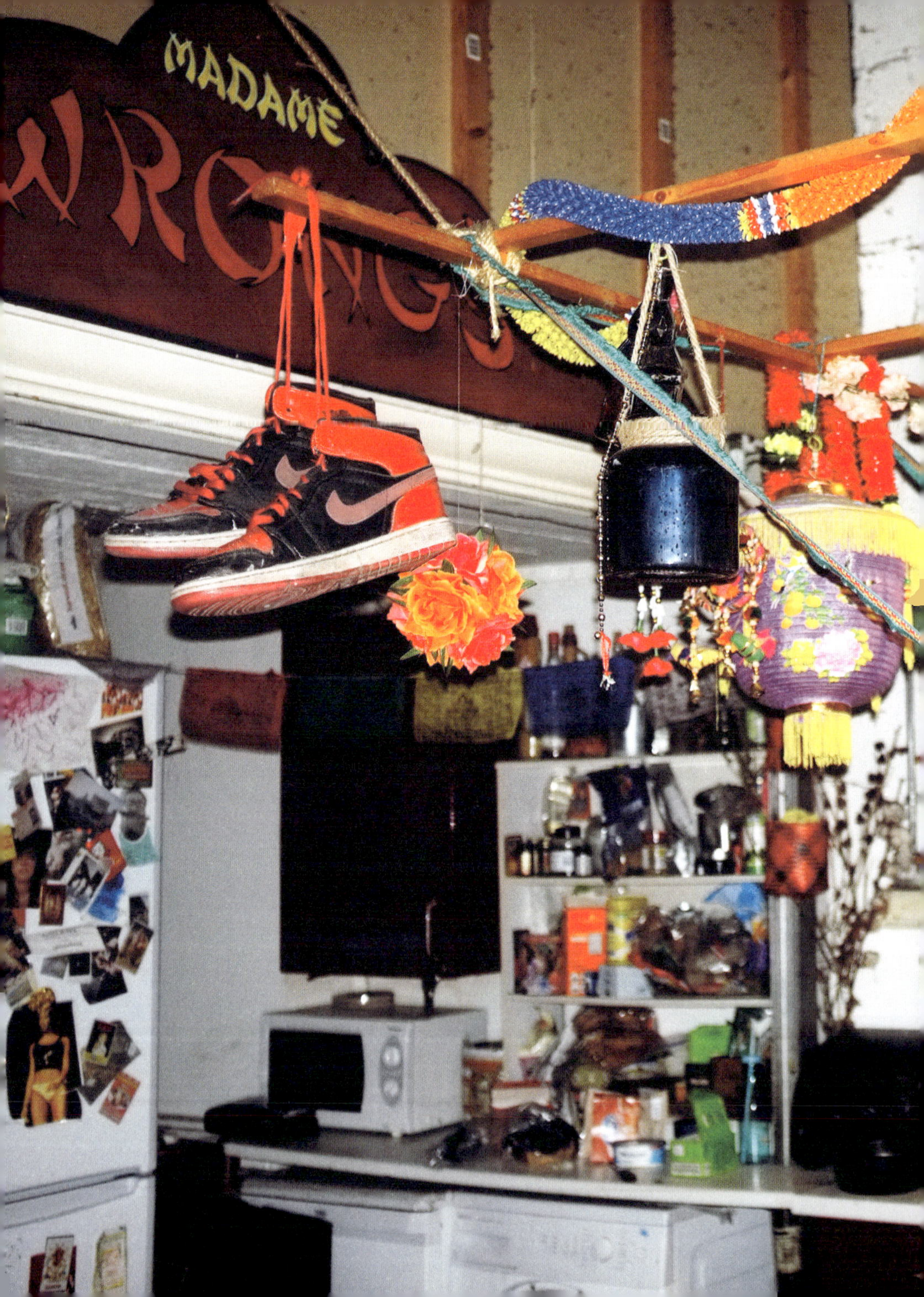
MADAME
WRONG

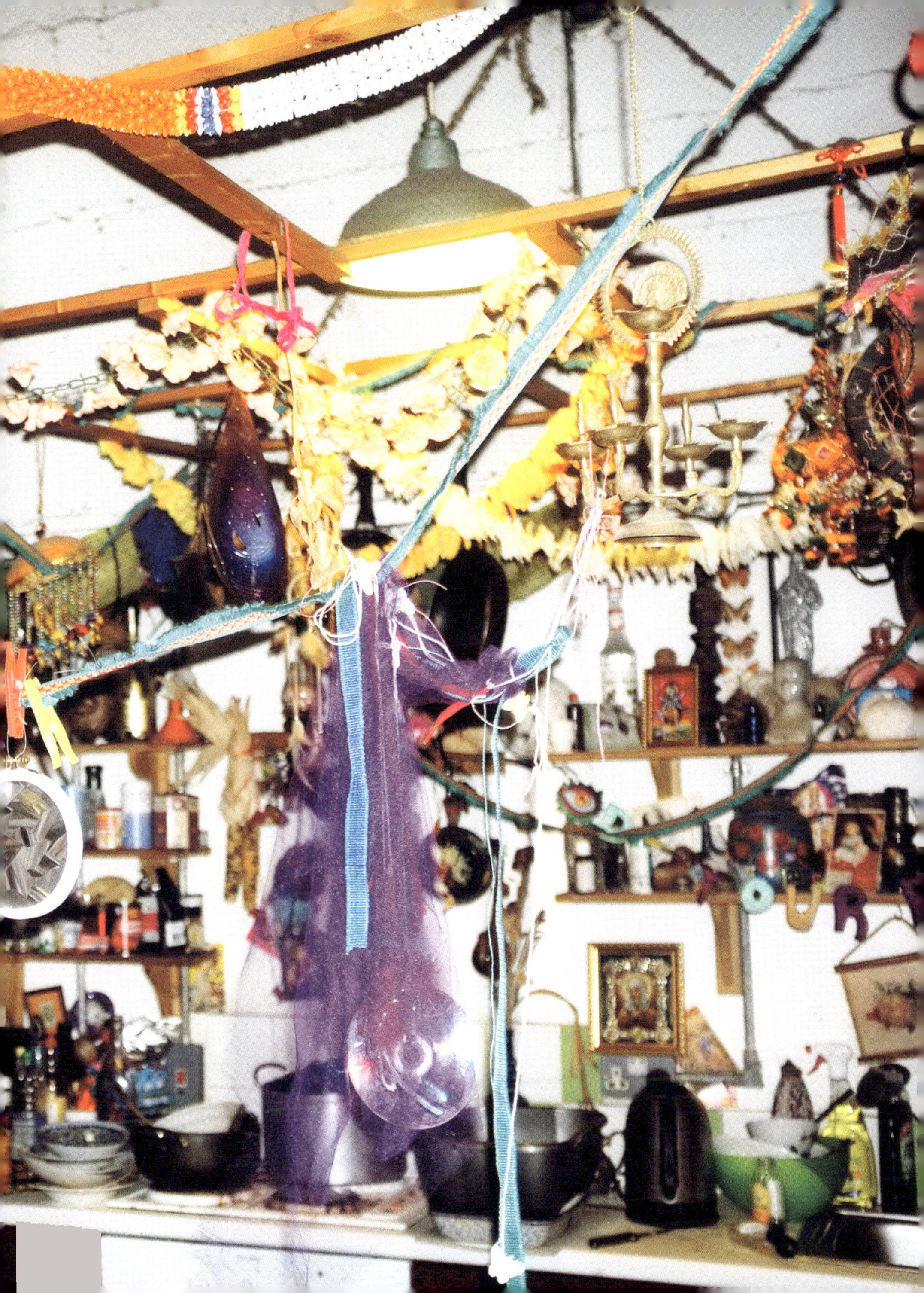

INTRODUCTION

When Iain McKell met a group of young female artists living in Tottenham, North London, he was struck by their 'sparkly personalities' and quirky dress sense. Colourful hair, Buffalo boots, ethnic jewellery and 1970s vintage leopard skin print flares: it all added up to a unique aesthetic that smacked of subculture, individuality, creativity; of women who know their own minds.

It was spring 2016 and Iain had recently moved from West to East London. On and off for two years, he spent time at the girls' warehouse and in the warehouses of their friends across the capital, documenting parties and everyday comings and goings, but also free festivals, pop-up events and art performances with which the girls were involved. Gradually, candid shots of spontaneous moments became a much deeper, collaborative body of work about a group of young adults – a sisterhood – exploring their identities, both individually and collectively.

The longer he spent with the girls and an extended network of artist-friends, the more inspired by their lifestyle and attitudes towards self-expression, art and collaboration Iain became. He had found himself, completely by chance, on a journey not dissimilar to those made in the past – as a teenager on a voyage of self-discovery in the 1970s documenting youth culture in his hometown of Weymouth ('Private Reality: The Diary of a Teenage Boy'), or as a young photographer in early 1980s London photographing the New Romantics ('Cult With No Name').

What this new body of work has in common with his earlier series is a desire by Iain to record, indeed, to 'tak[e] up that singularly photographic opportunity to be involved [with] and yet remain "outside"' an alternative culture, as Val Williams, the photography writer and curator, aptly puts it. In the project that would become *New Girl Order,* Iain played with reality as it unfolded around him, finding ways to blend real life with fiction. This manifested as organised shoots or set-up shots alongside in-the-moment photographs captured by chance.

Looking at the work as a whole it is often difficult to tell what has been constructed and what has not, but this is precisely what Iain is getting at; life is art and art is life – the two are inextricably entwined, at least for these women. What Iain gives us is a sense of performance, or rather, what it means to perform oneself – as an artist, and ultimately, as a human being.

The work is, on the one hand, very much of its time, a 21st century portrait of a 'community of feisty individualistic females who share a unique, strong and loving bond', to quote Iain. Indeed, he has said that all of his work reflects, like a mirror, the time in which it is made and always comes from a personal point of view. But it could also be said that *New Girl Order* transcends a particular time and place, for who hasn't experienced a period of self-discovery or felt the thrill and sheer joy of being part of a group of like-minded souls.

Whether it's a quiet moment of contemplation or mischievous merrymaking, Iain's images remind us that it's OK to embrace the most creative parts of who we are and to follow where our desire for self-expression leads.

Gemma Padley
London, 2019

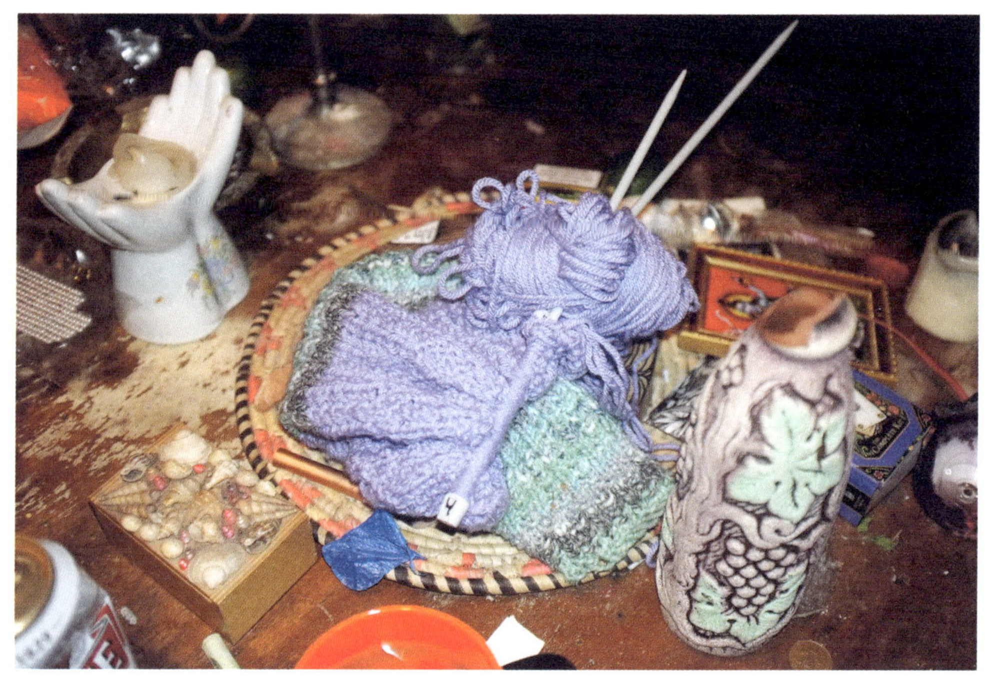

THANKS

Thanks to the Sisterhood (aka 'Siblinghood') for their collaboration and generosity, without which none of this would have been possible: Ayesha Tan Jones, Camilla Mason, Charis Bee, Ellie Walker, Ely Howard, Grace Mulligan, Heather Stewart, Jemima Nell, Jess Christenson, Kitty Juby, Shanti Goupil and Tish Walker.

To all the other gals, guys and pals of the Sisterhood who I met and/or photographed along the way and those who feature in the book: Debbie Stanton, Zia Sapphire Aurora, Darryn Sorensenbrowne, Monty Richthofen, Pedro Manuel Santos Moreira De Carvalho, Ella Lynch, Steph Coles, Nicole Paskauskas, Laura Gwyneth Butler, Joya Berrow, Daijour, Daniel, Po, Lily, Lauren and Muddled Miranda.

To Salon friends and family: Alice Hawkins, Matthew Finn, Dafydd Jones, Homer Sykes, David Moore, Jazz Willson, Dougie Wallace, Tom Sheperd, Julian Woollatt, Derek Ridgers, Malcom Gaskin, my daughter Jasmine McKell, my sister Jane McKell and my nephew Joseph Butcher. Scans by BDI and Ben White at Blaze. Everyone at Hoxton Mini Press and Friederike Huber for her beautiful editing and design.

Iain McKell
London, 2019

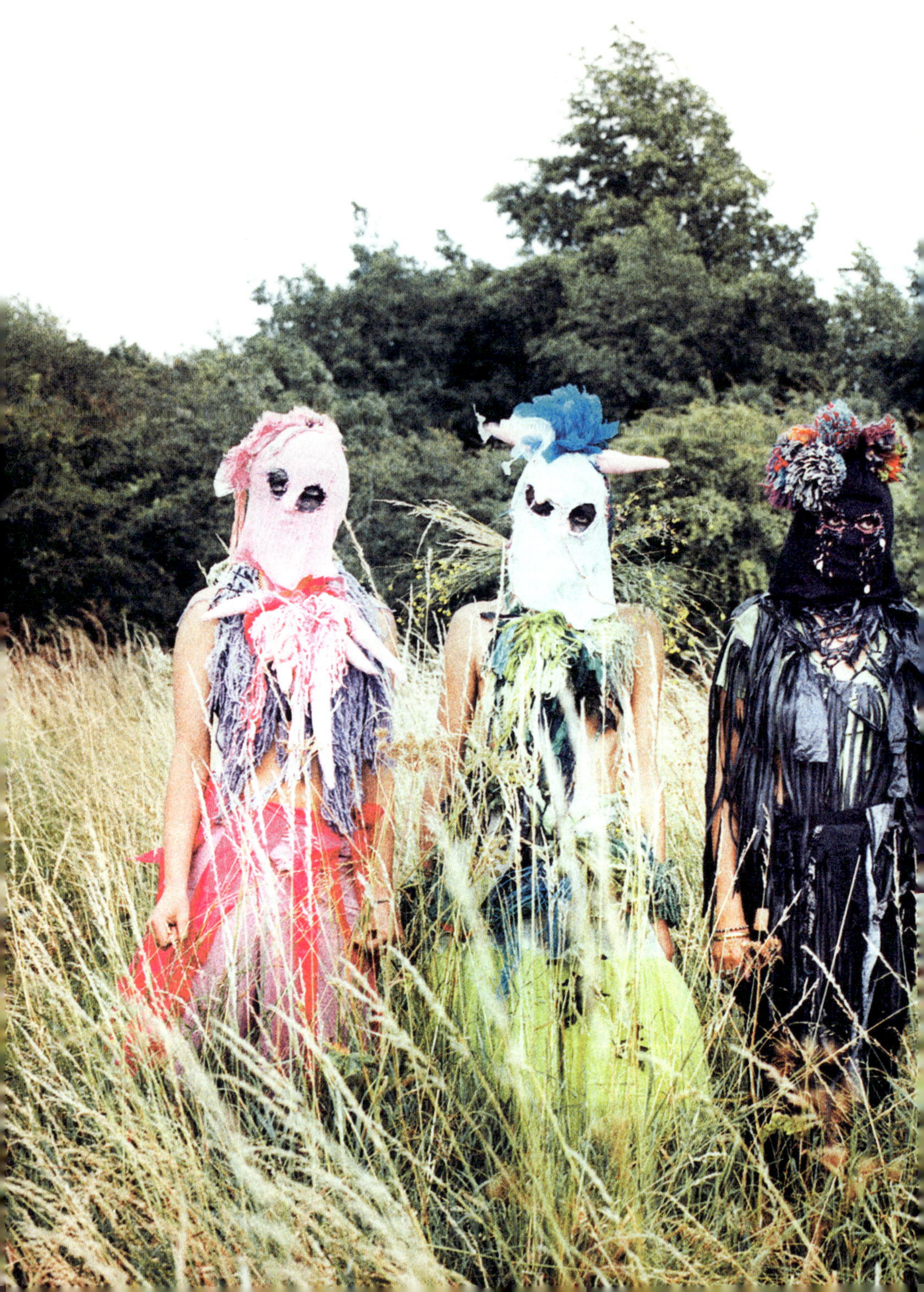

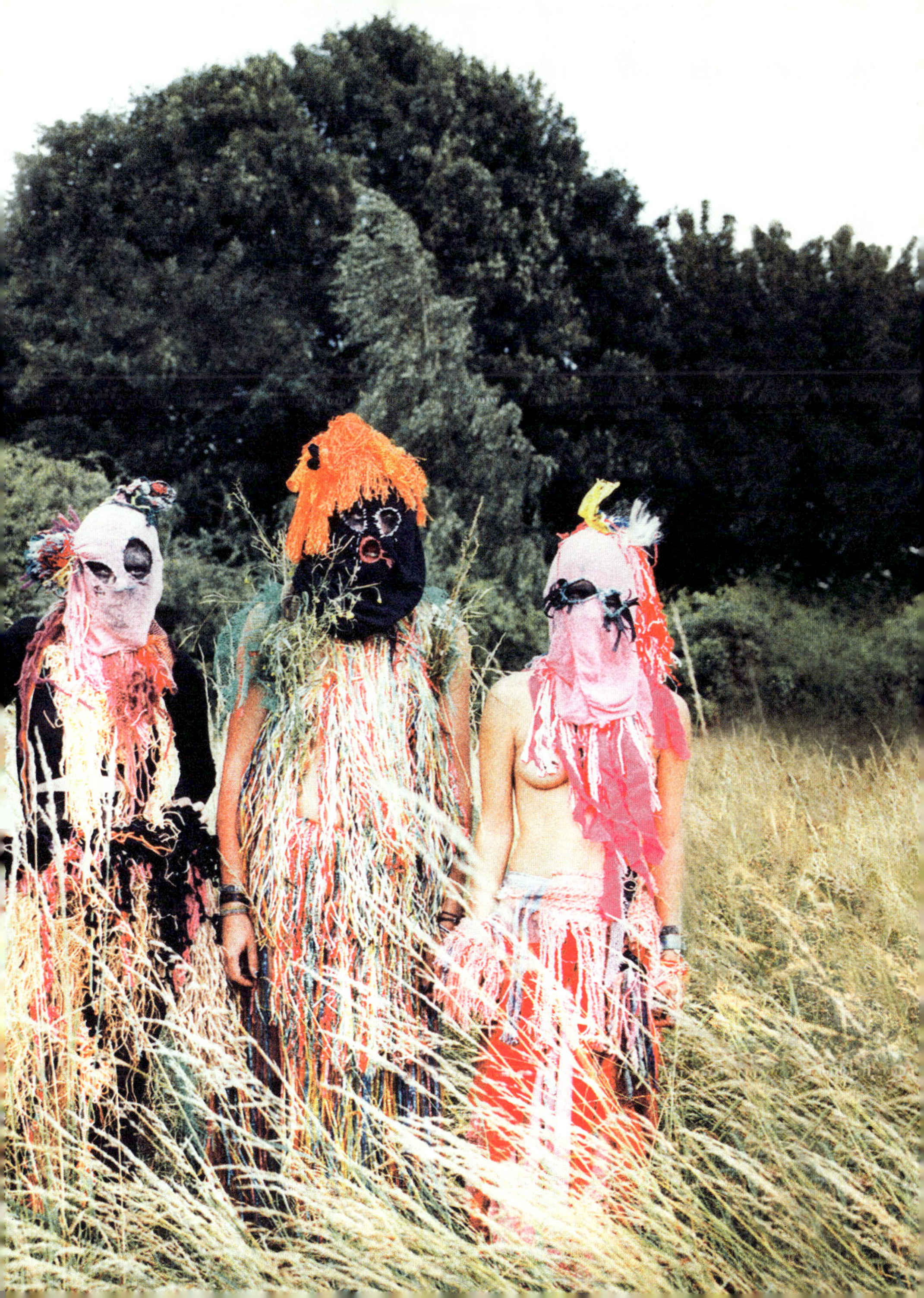

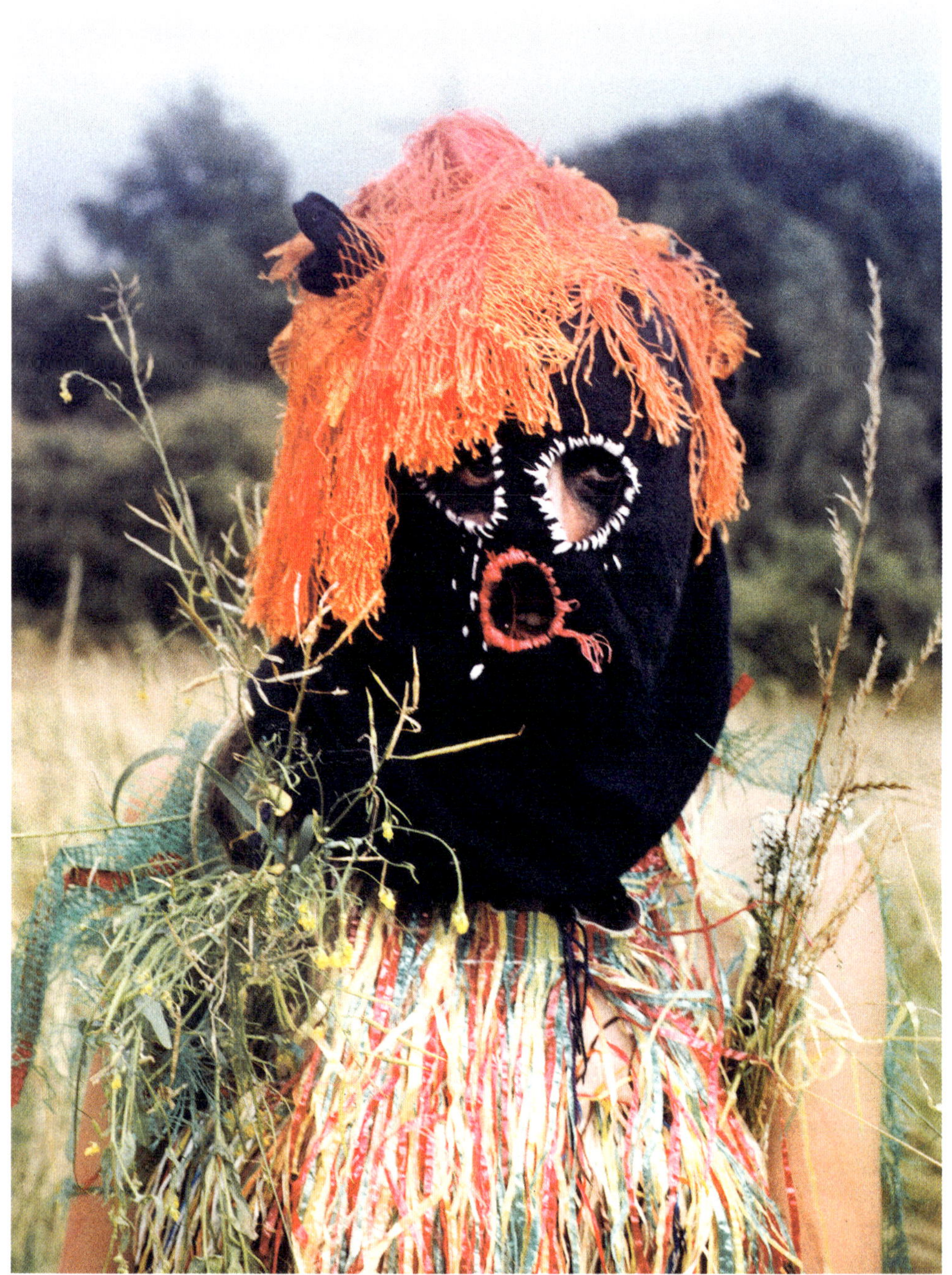

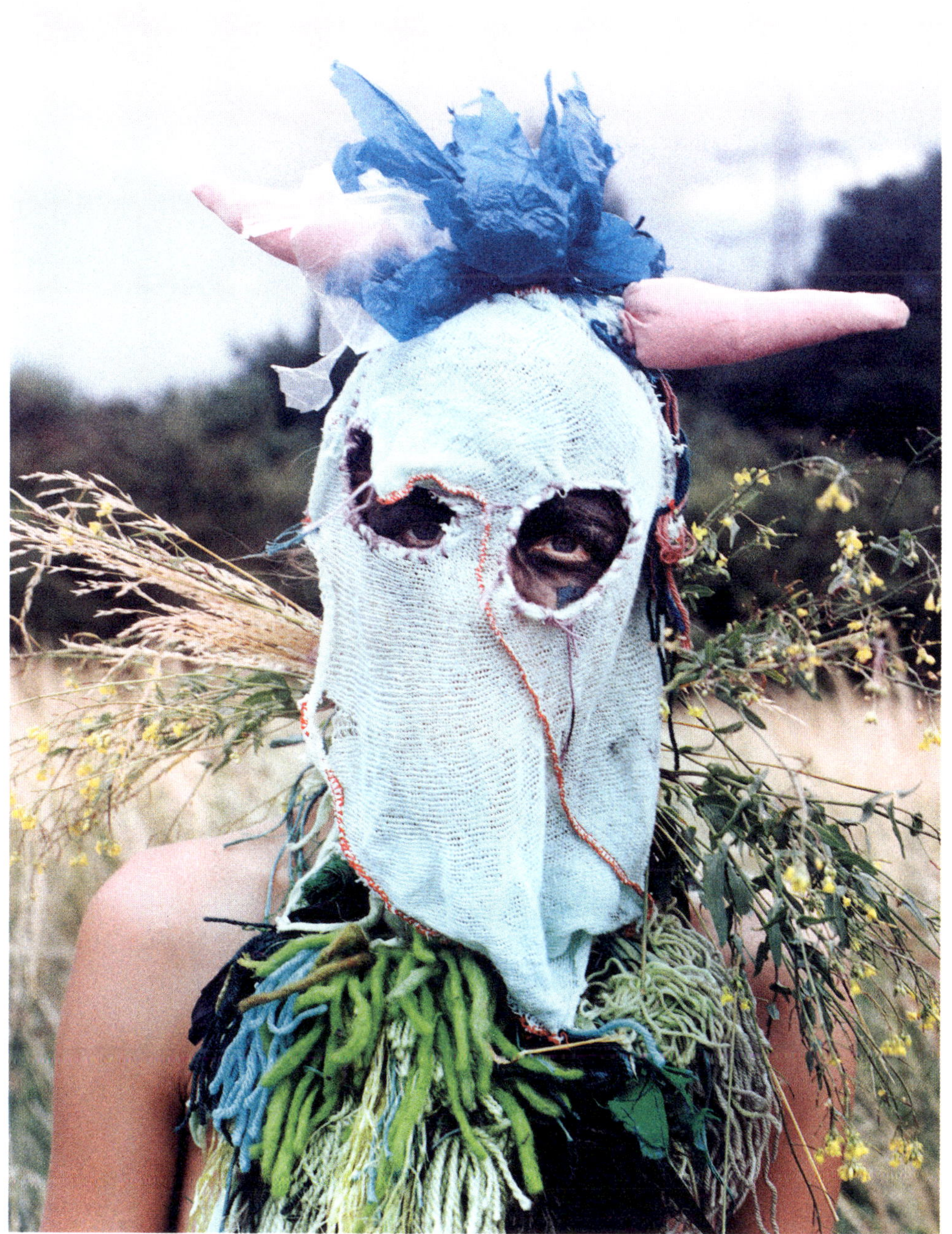

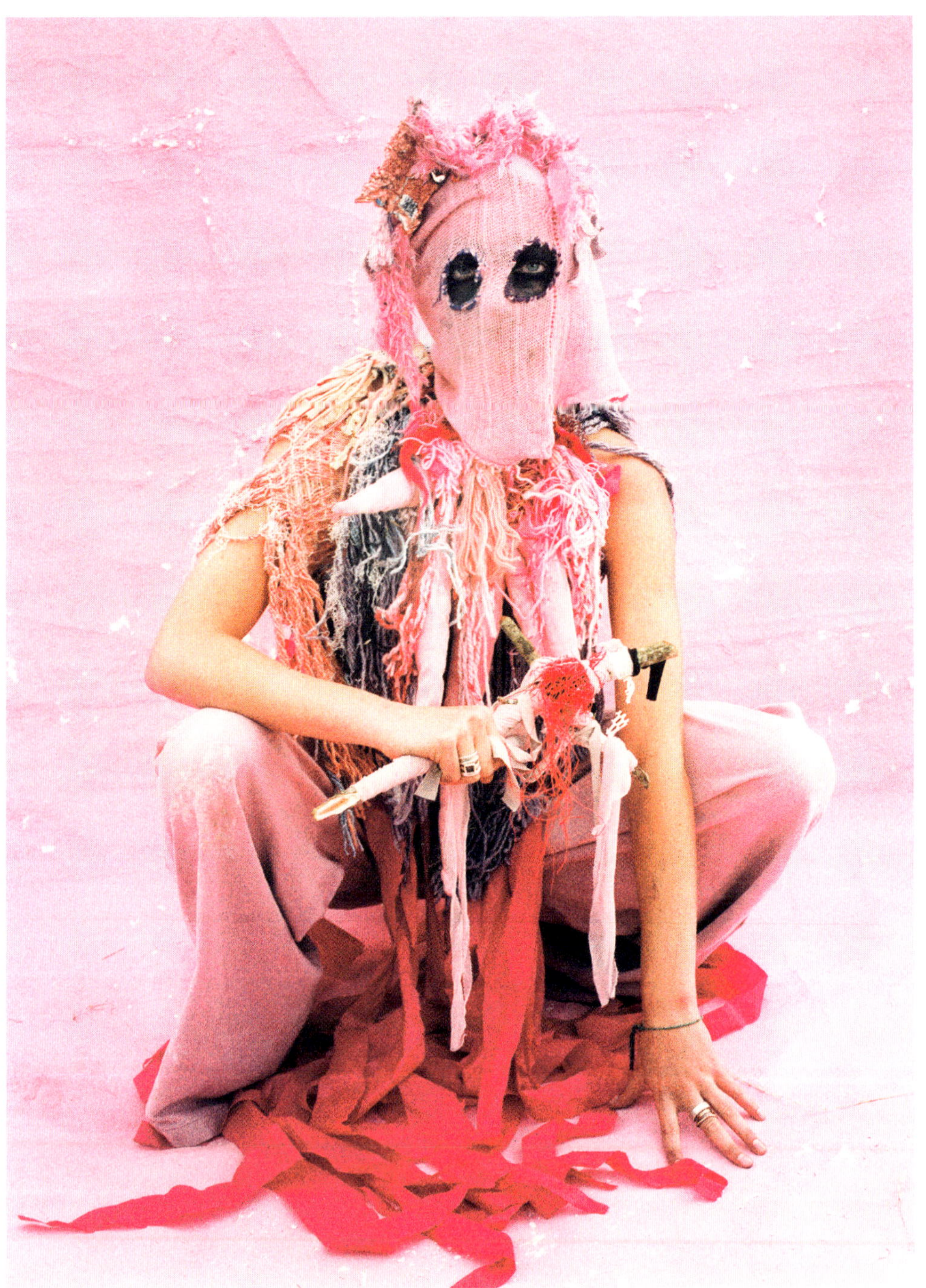

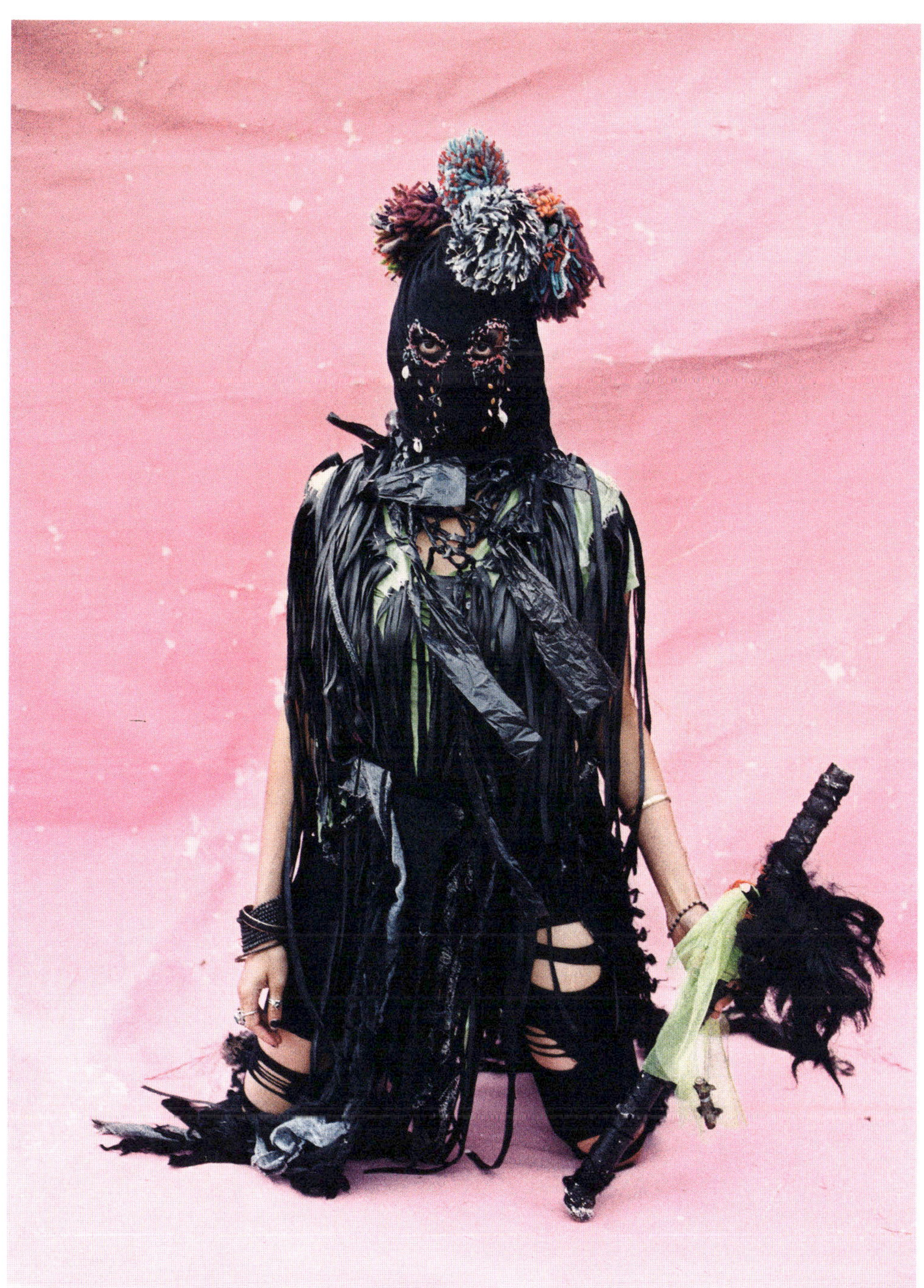

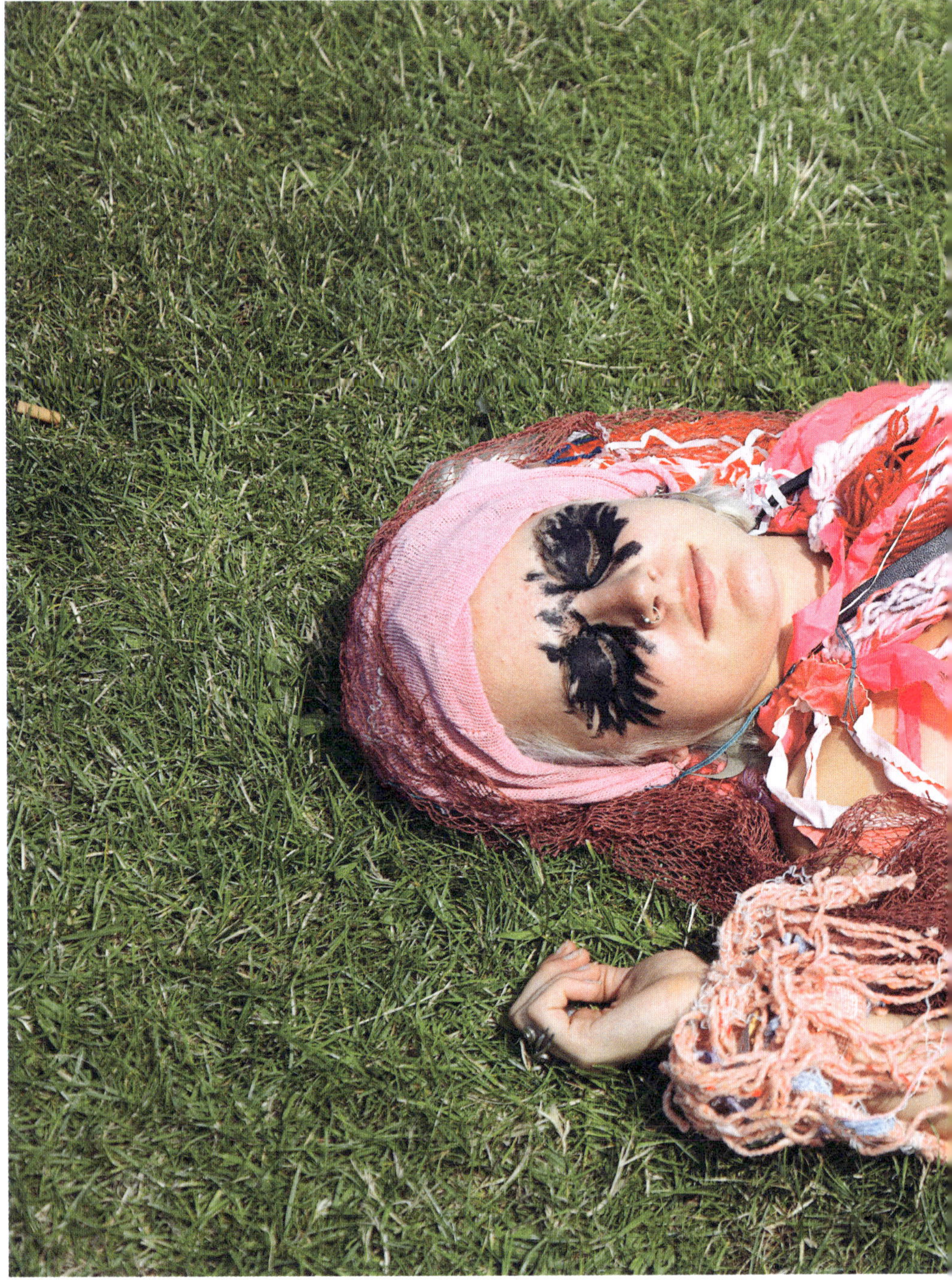

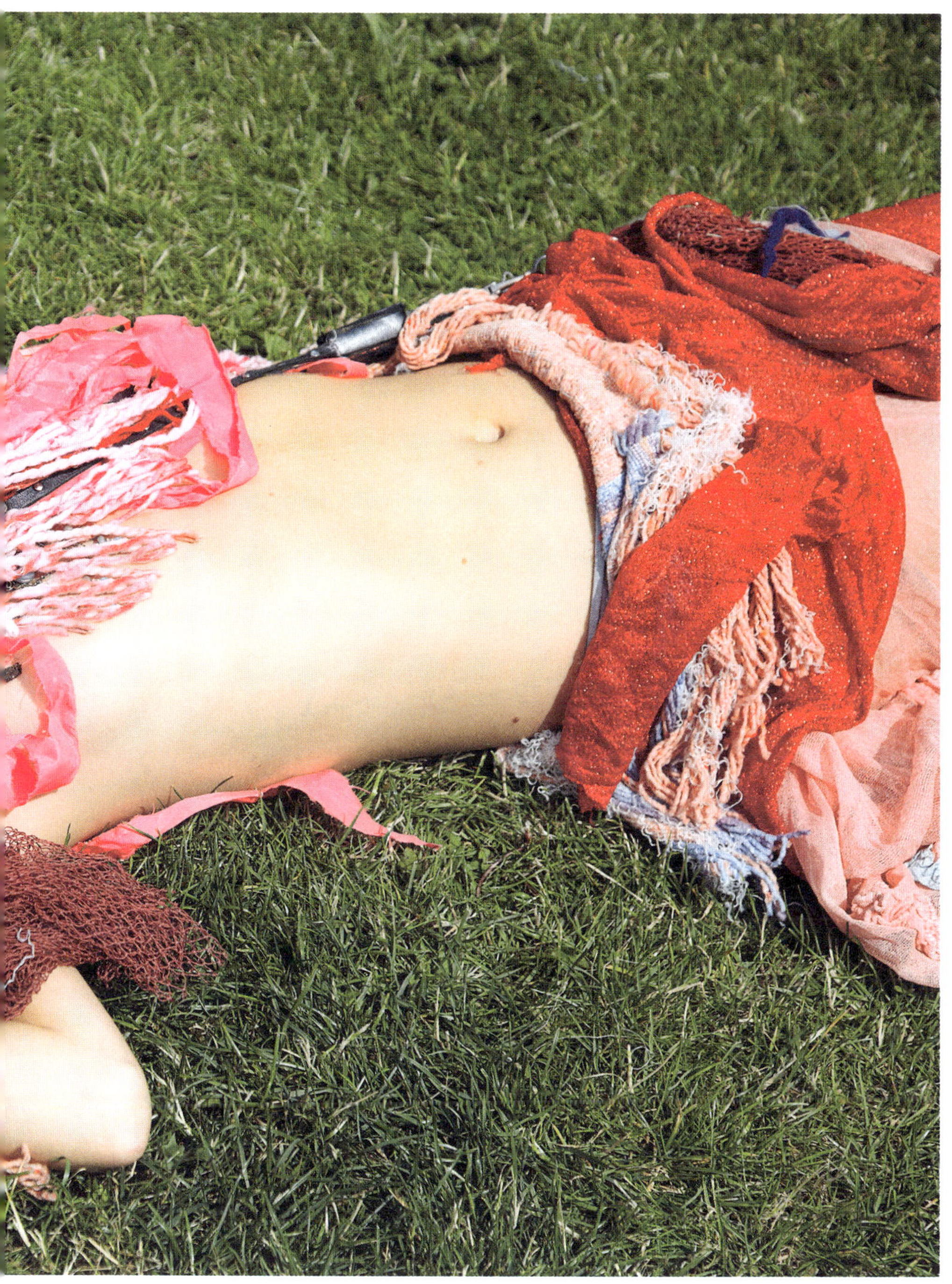

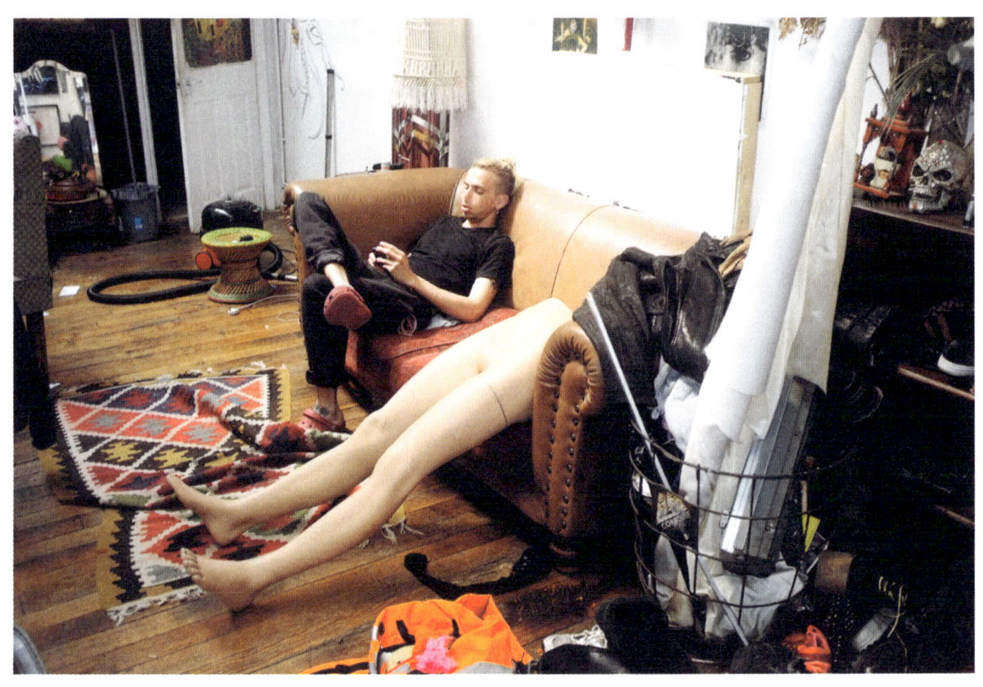

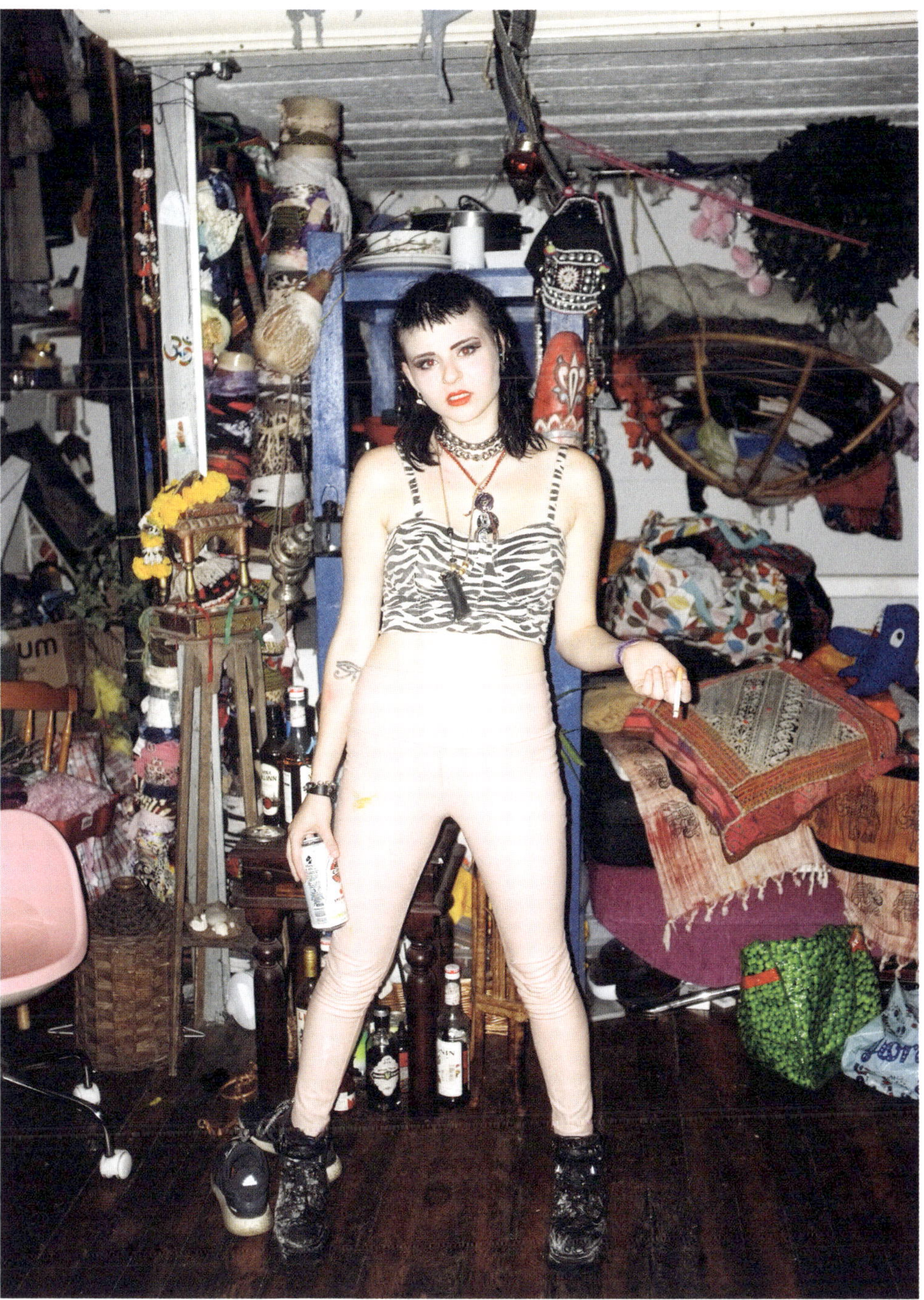

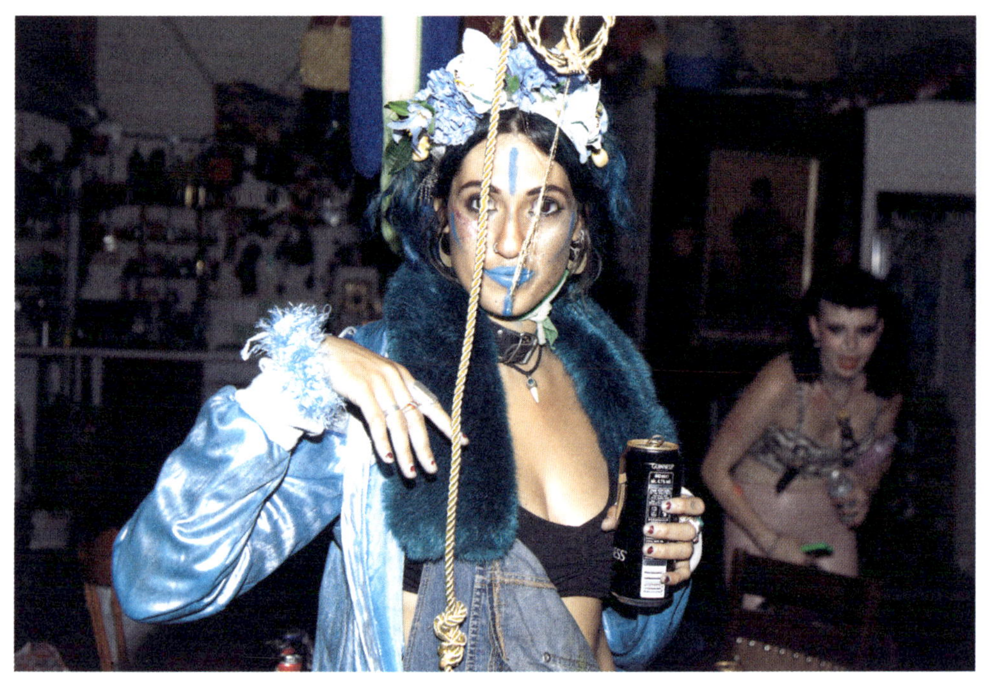

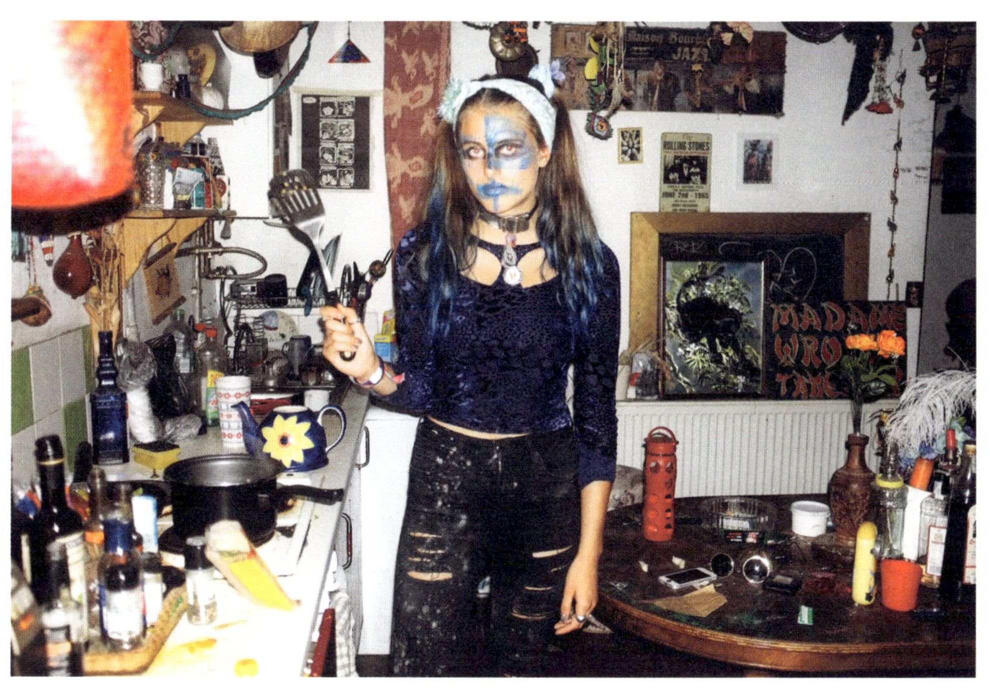

ROLLING STONES
JUNE 2nd · 1965
MADAME
WRO
TAB

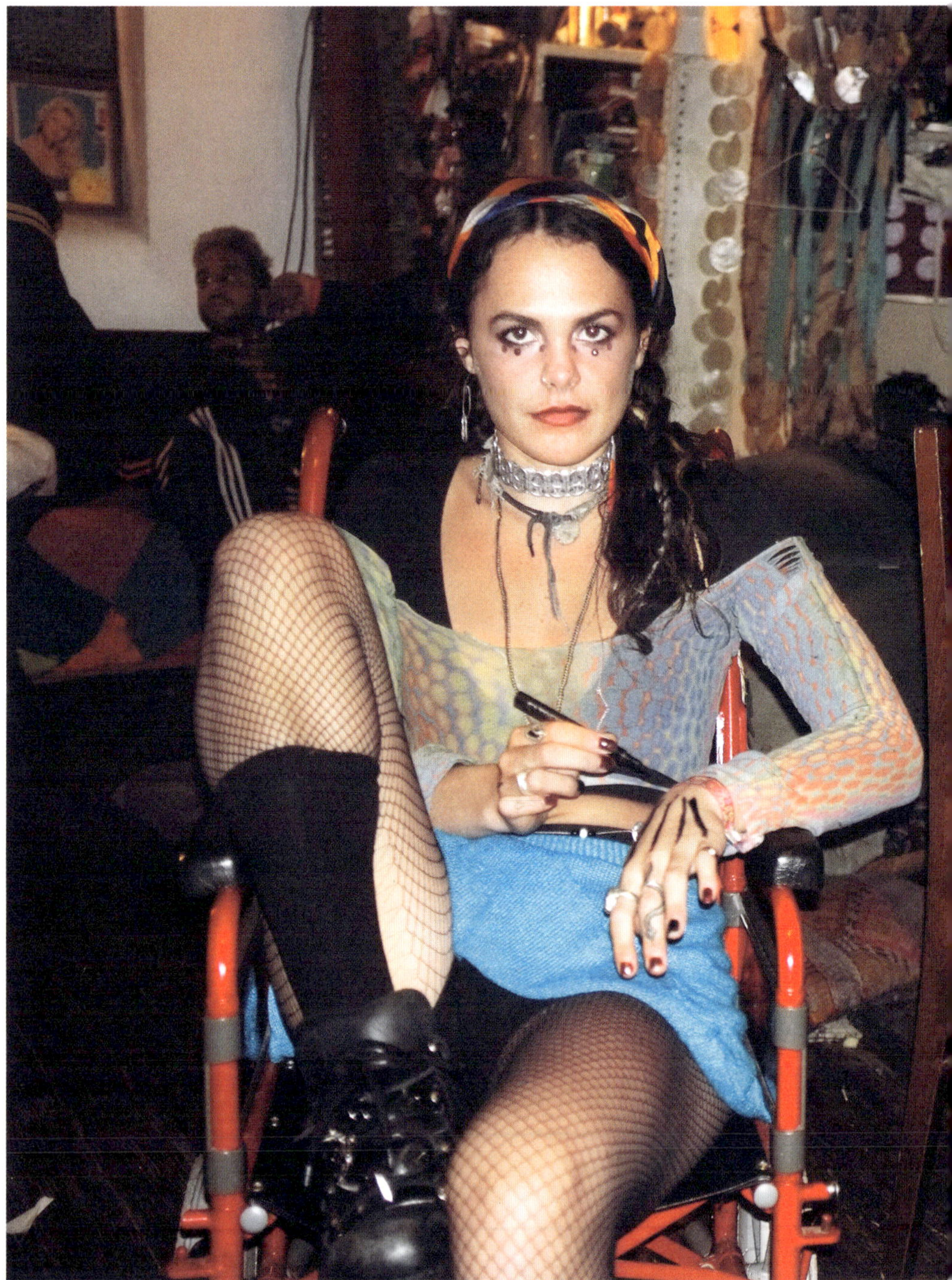

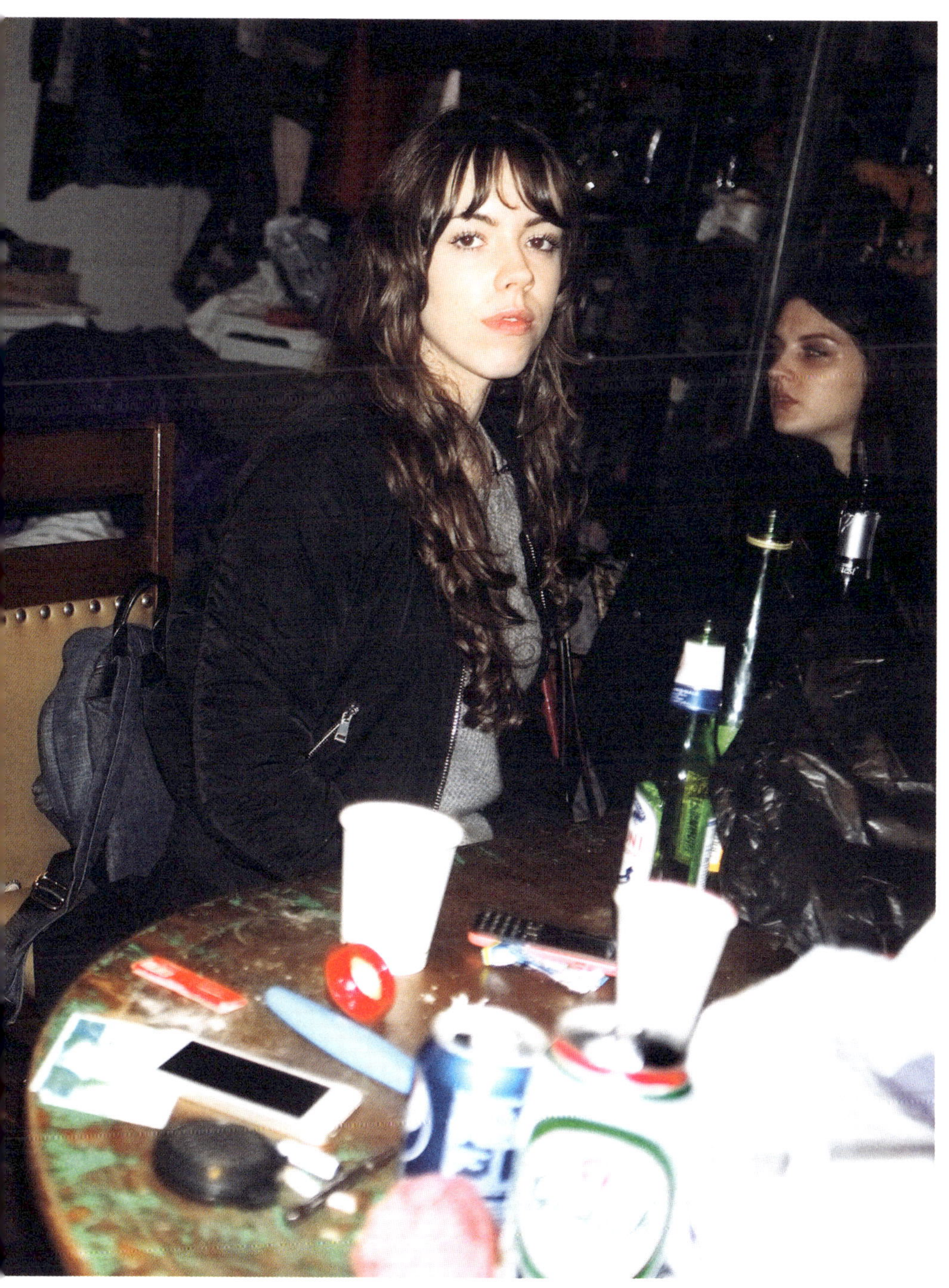

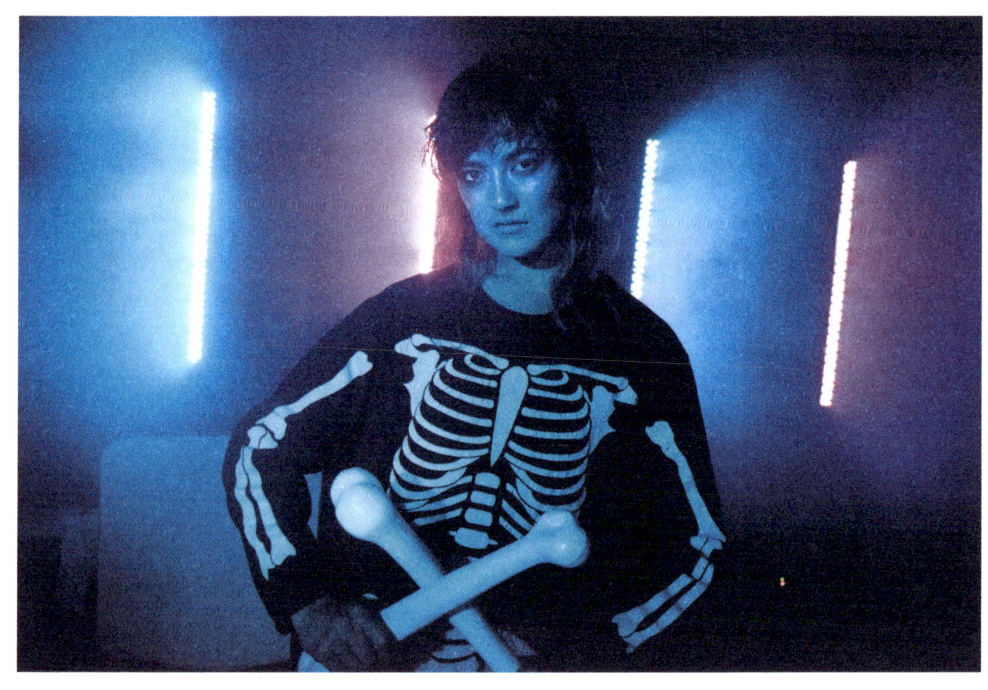

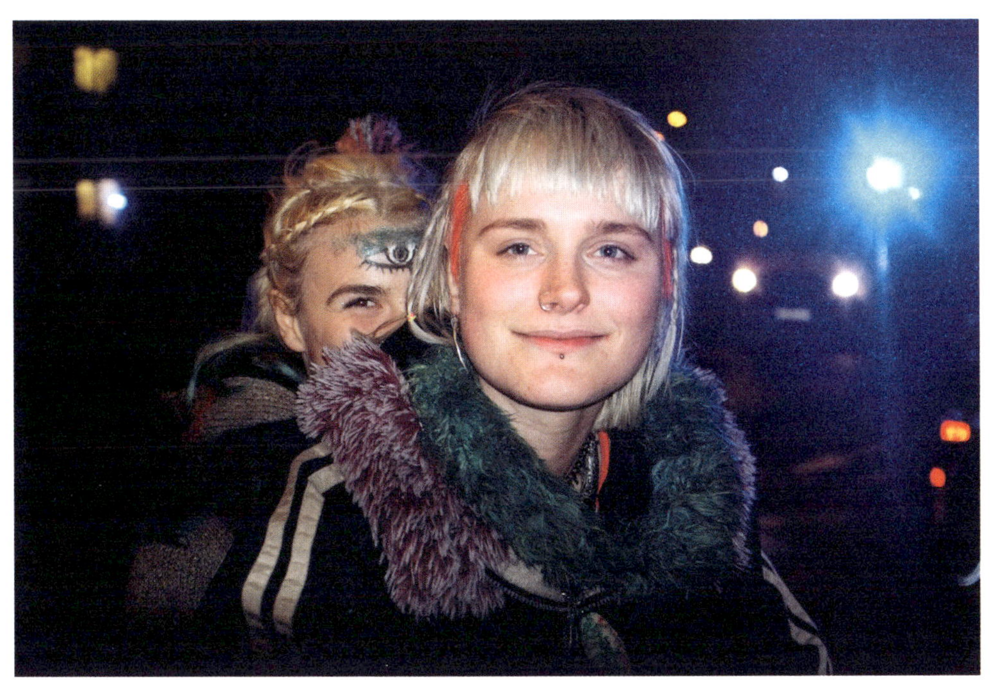

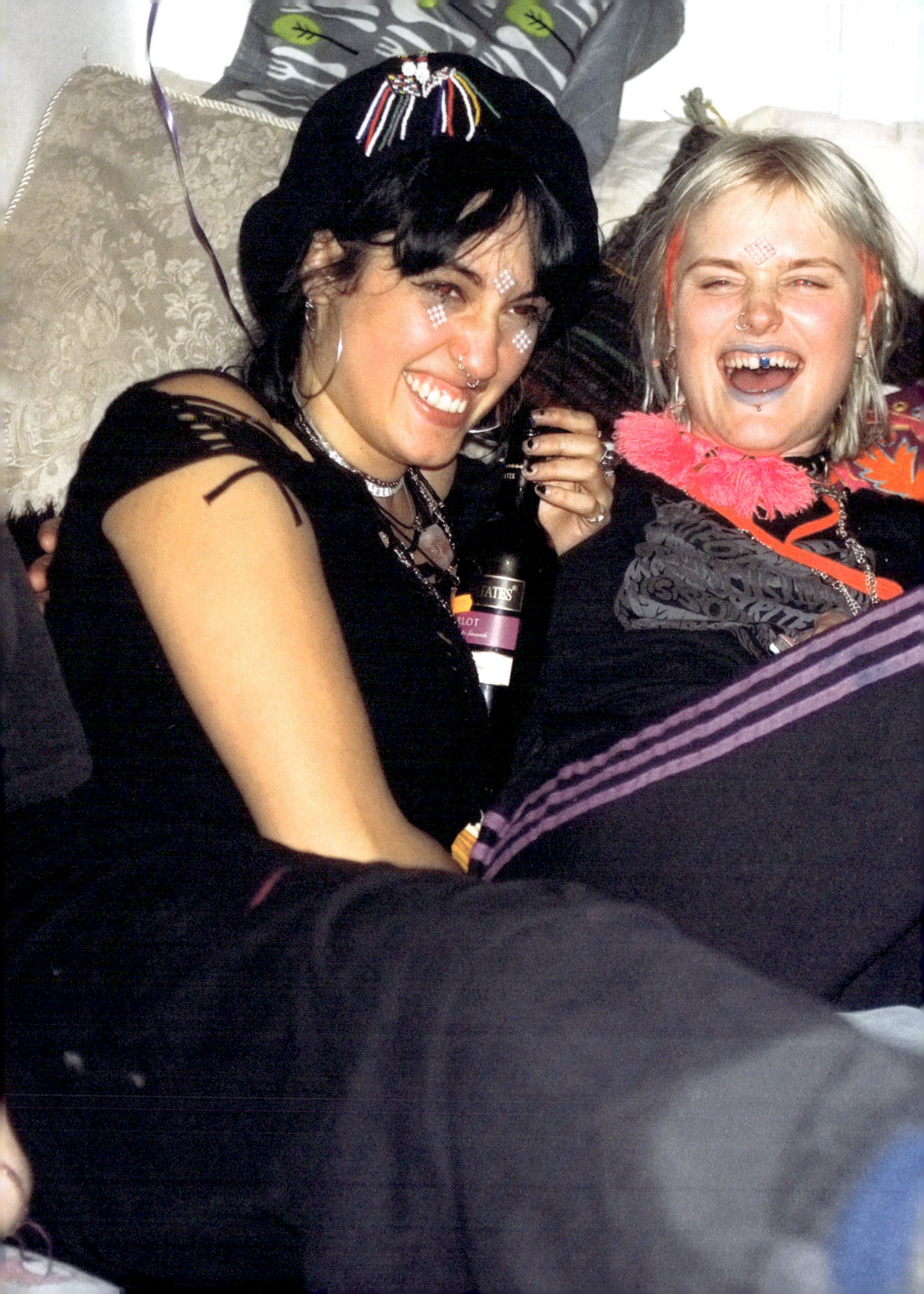

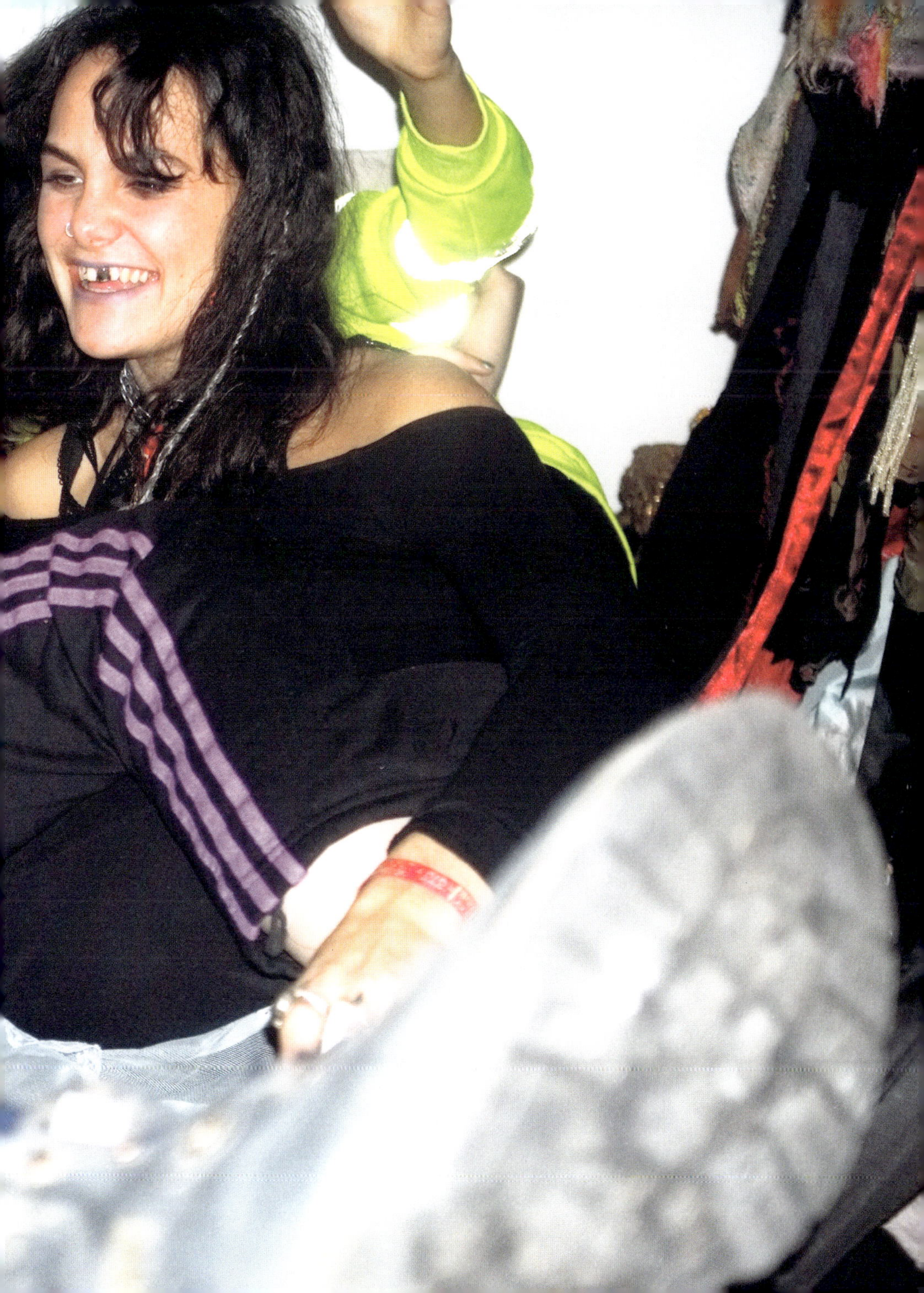

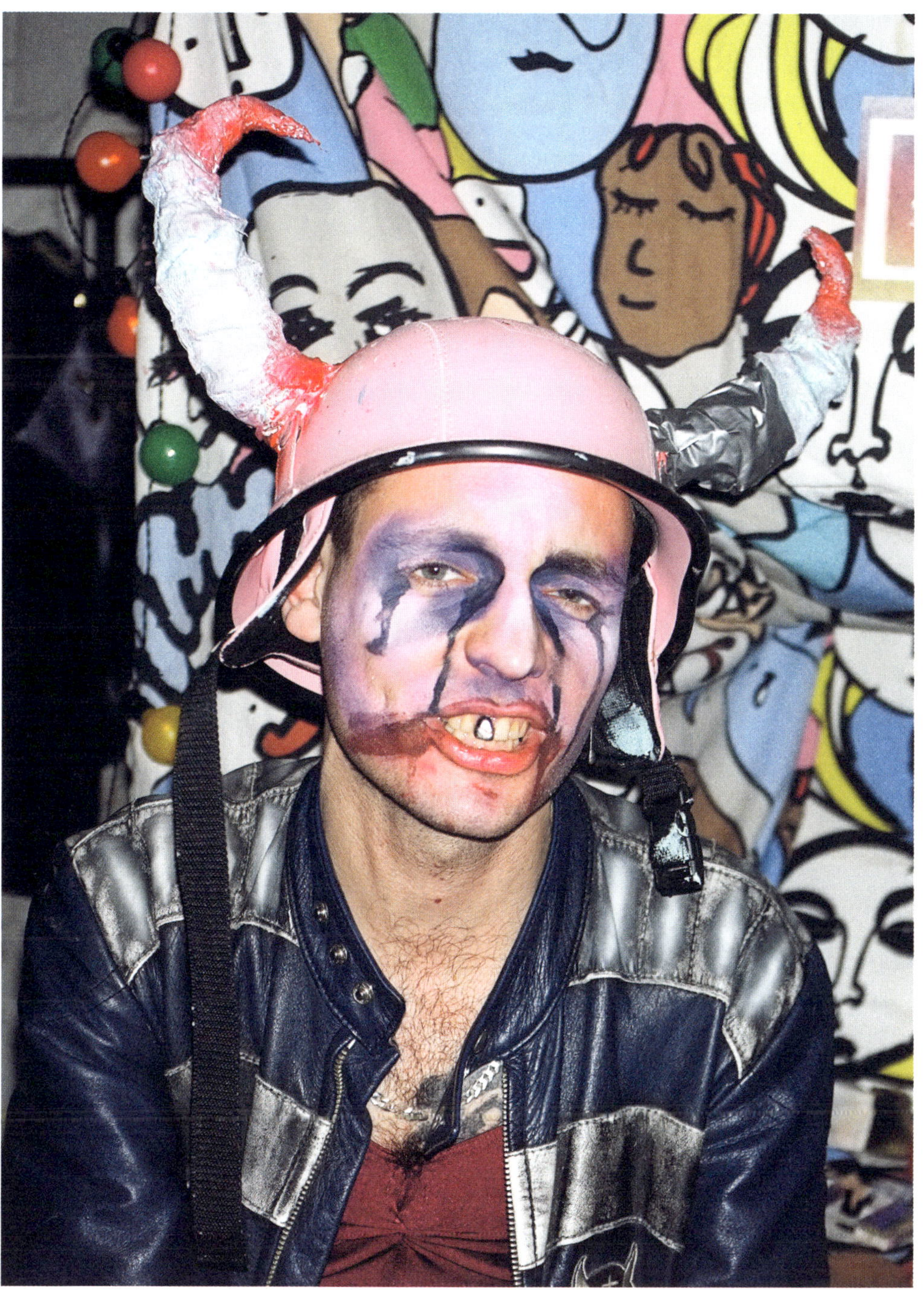

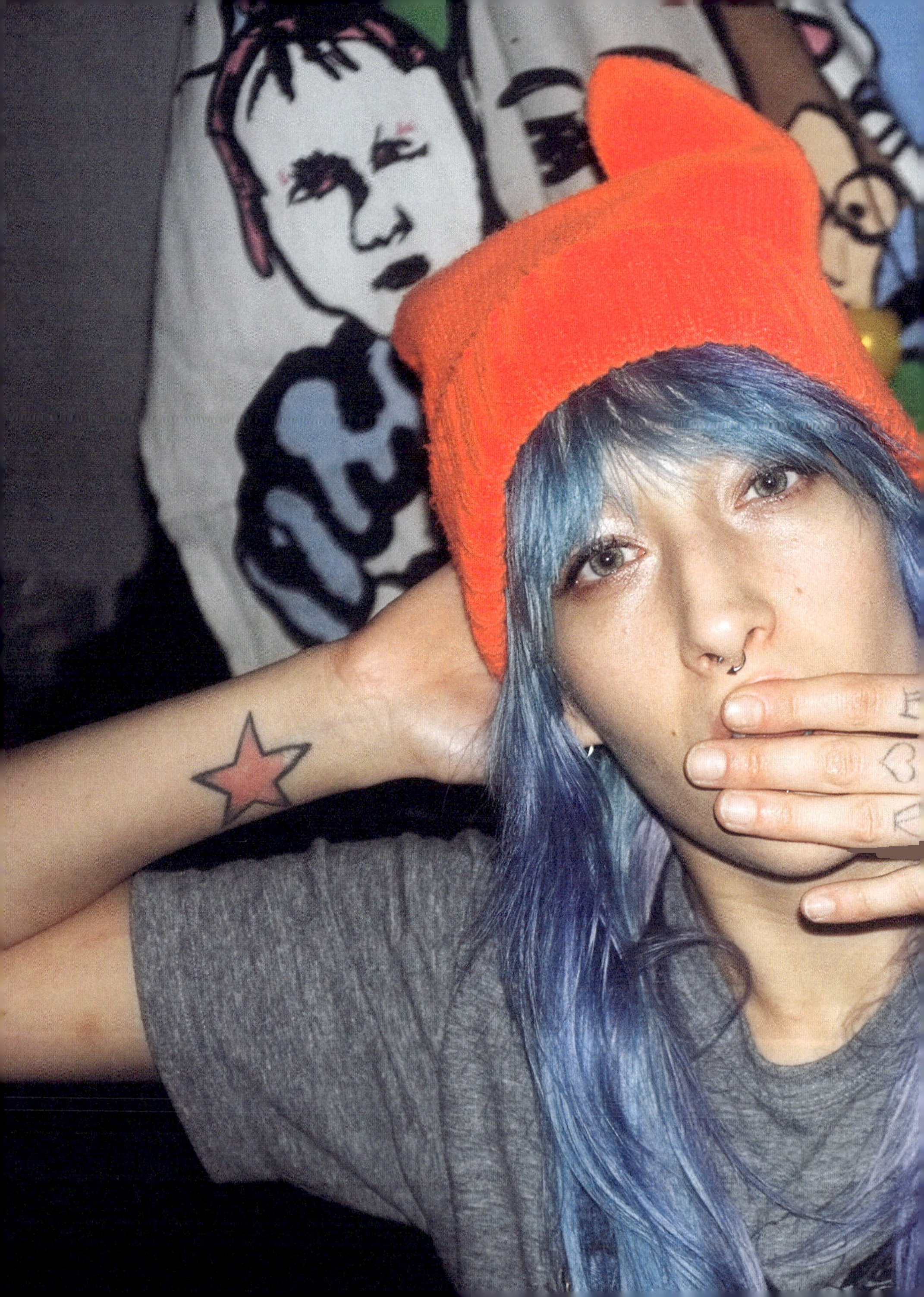

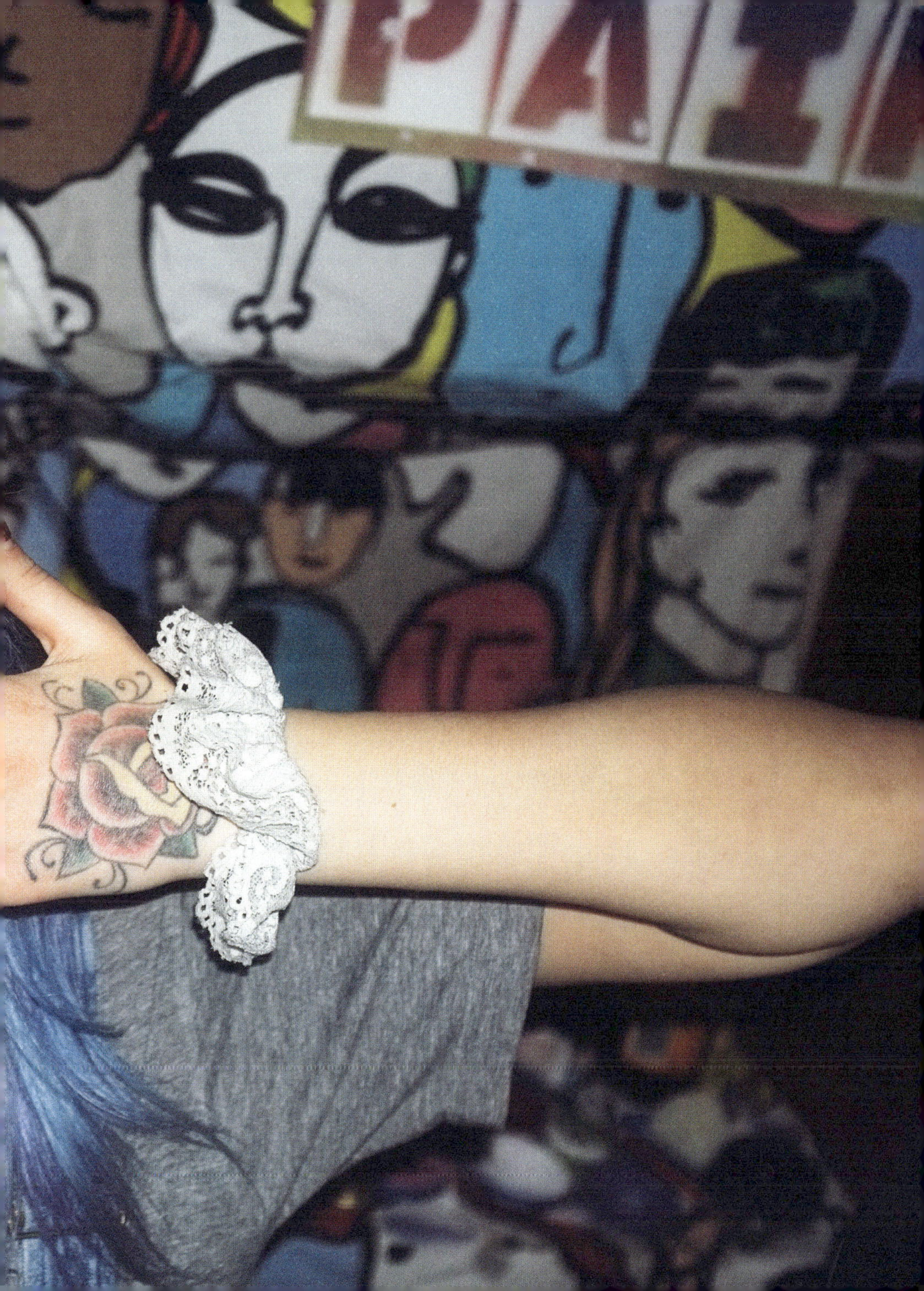

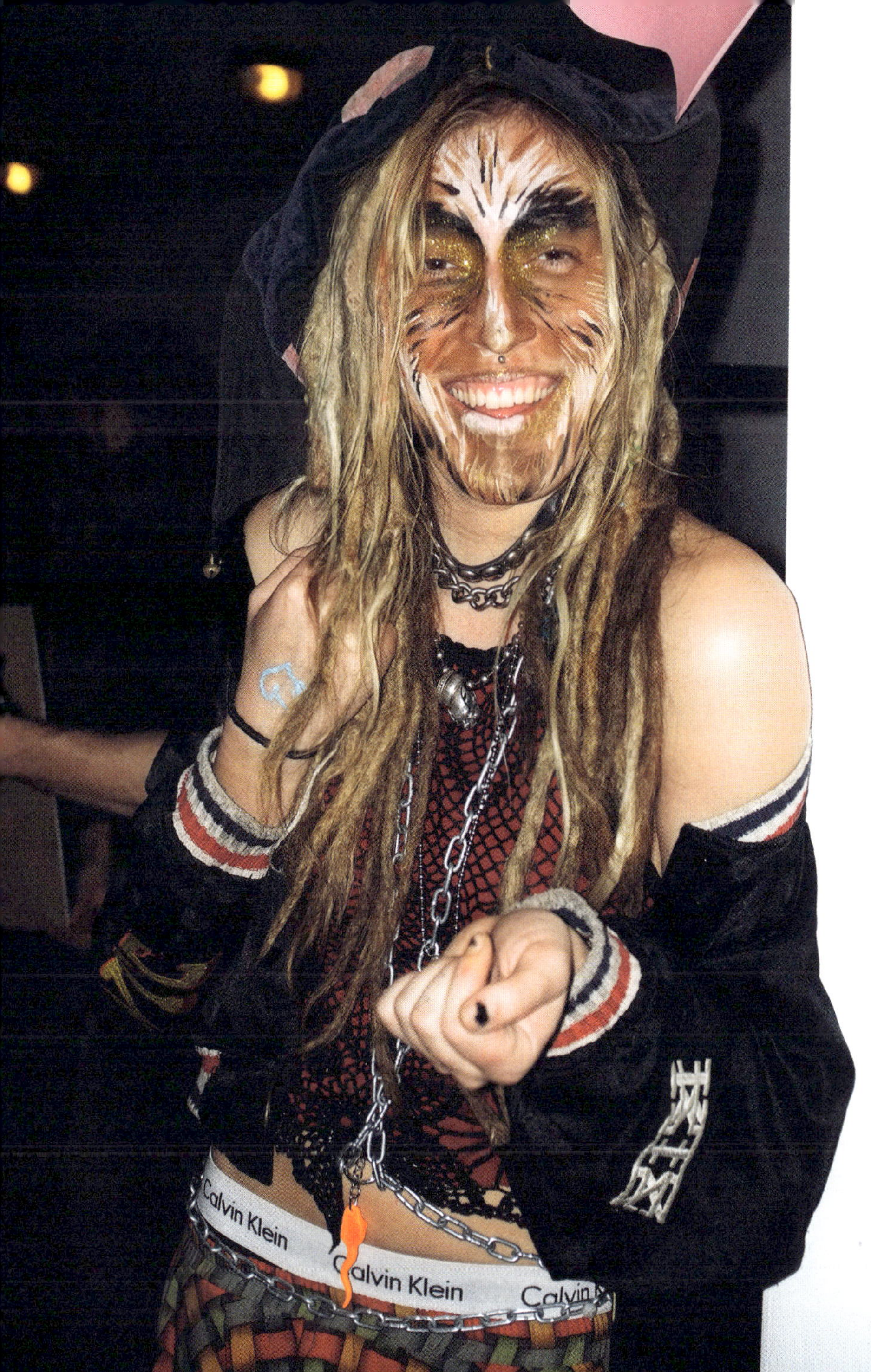

Calvin Klein
Calvin Klein
Calvin Klein

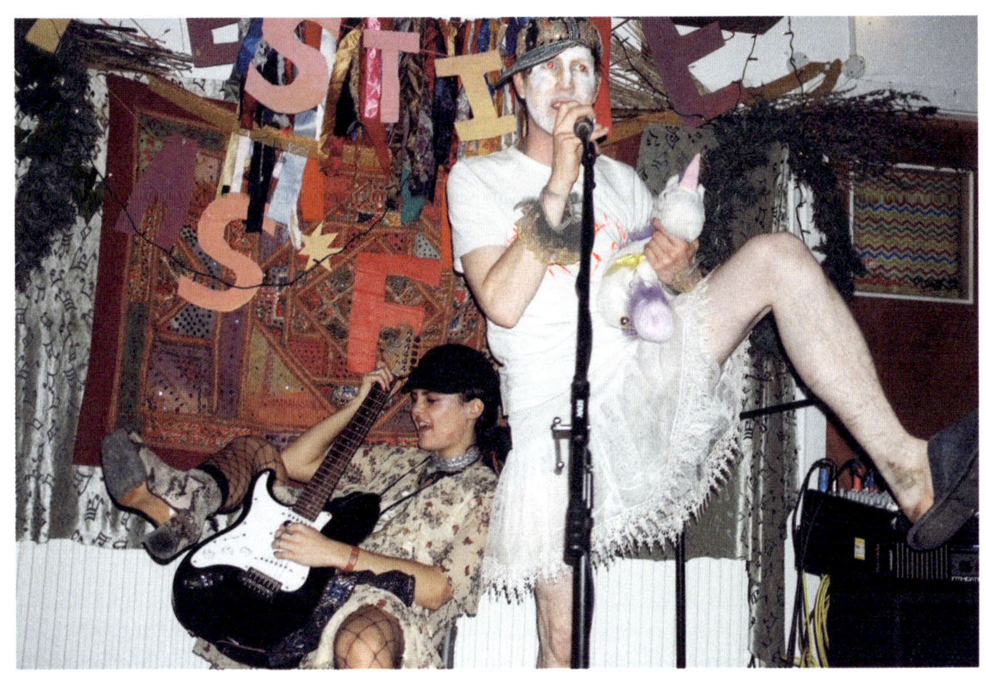

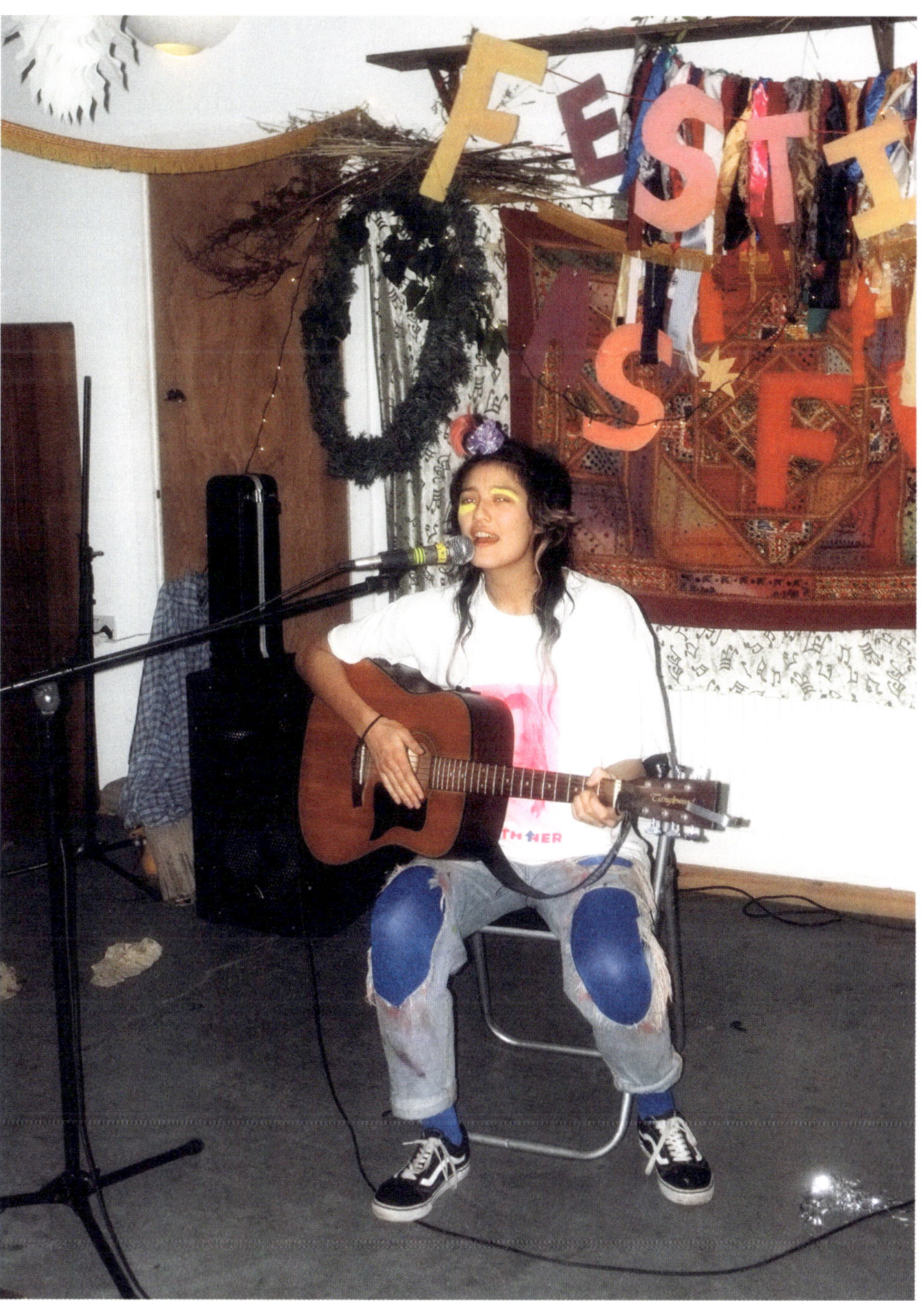

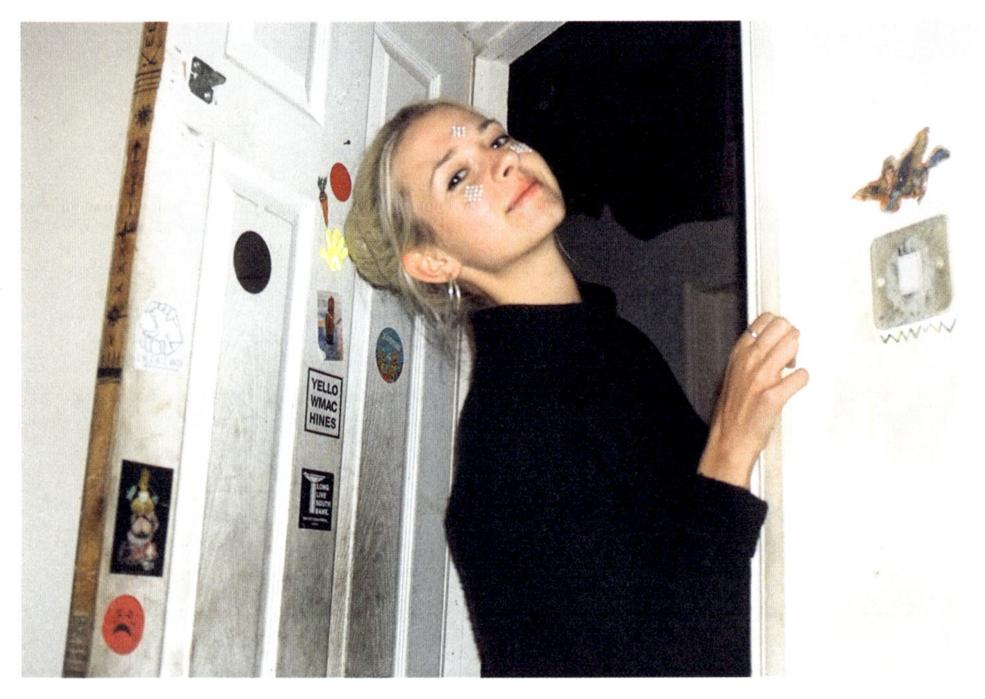

YELLO
WMAC
HINES
LONG
LIVE
SOUTH
BANK

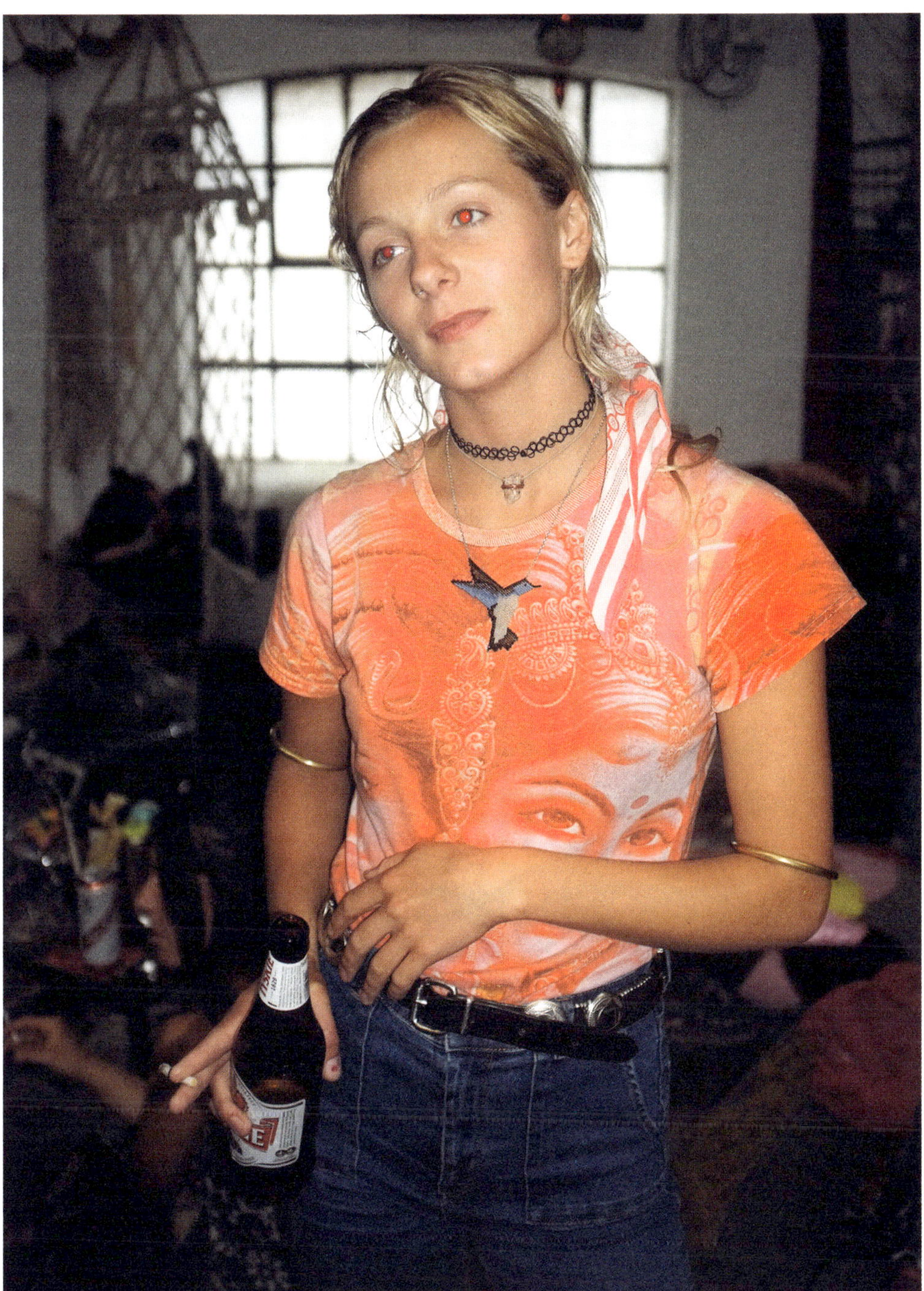

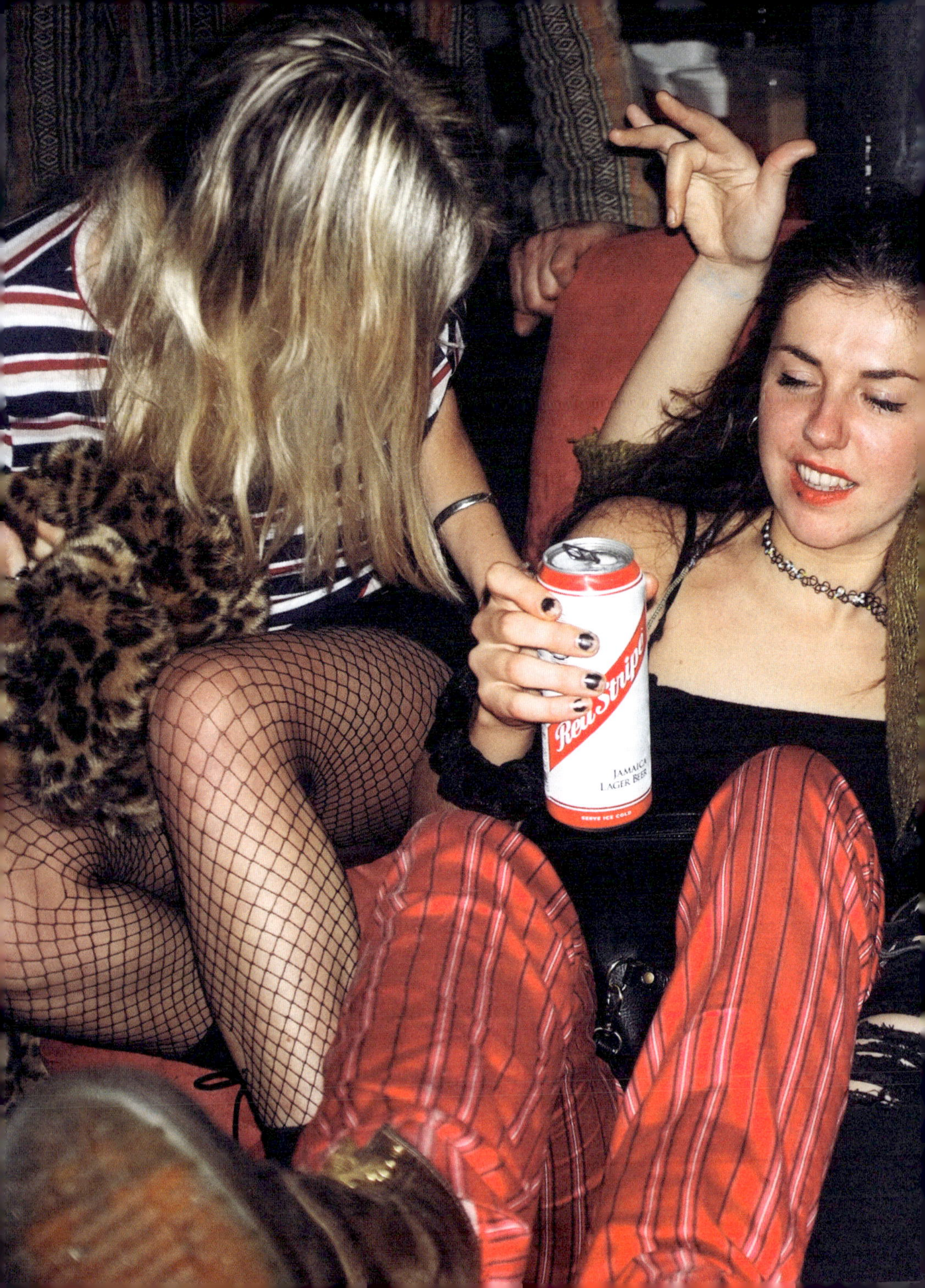
Red Stripe
JAMAICA
LAGER BEER
SERVE ICE COLD

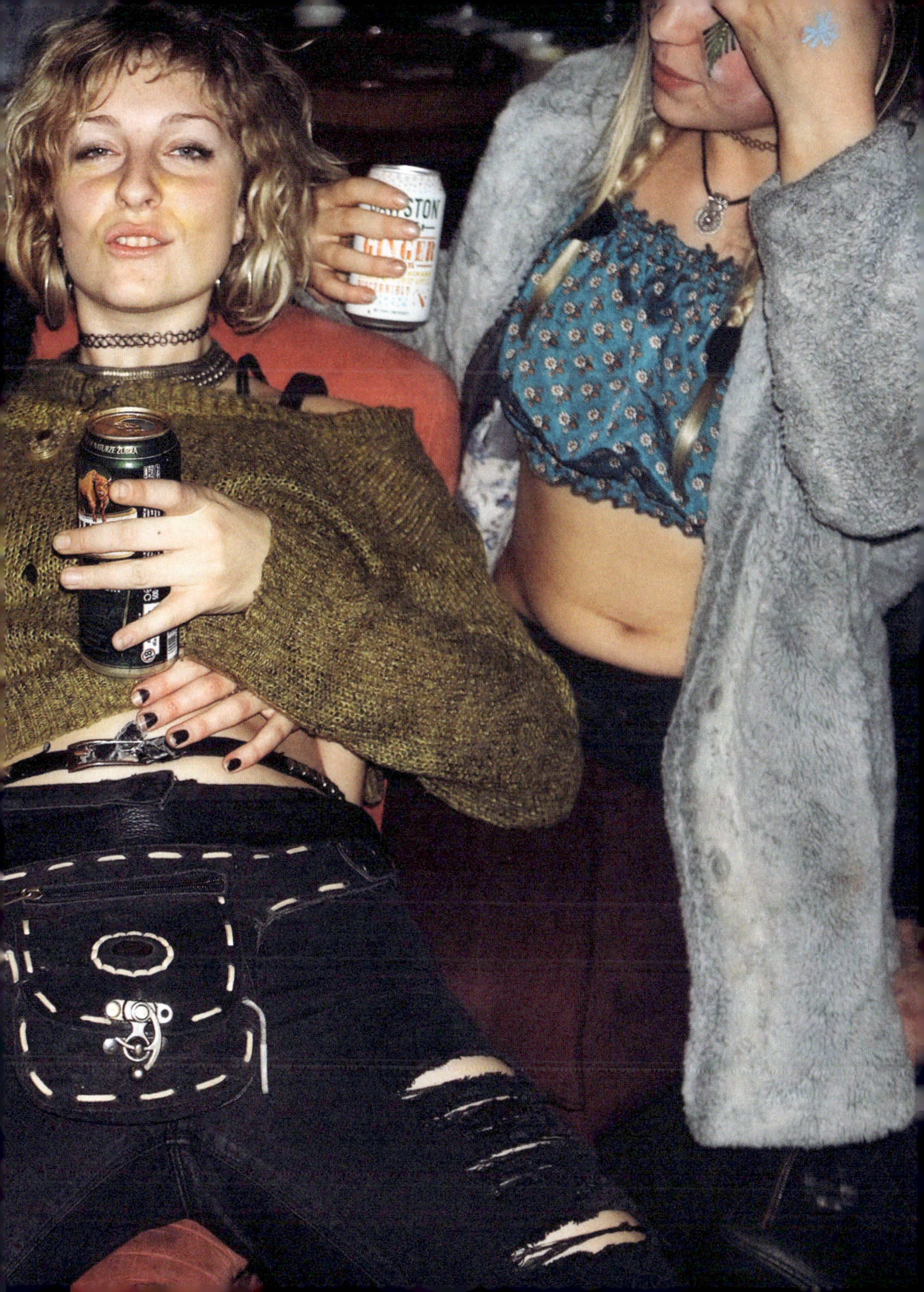

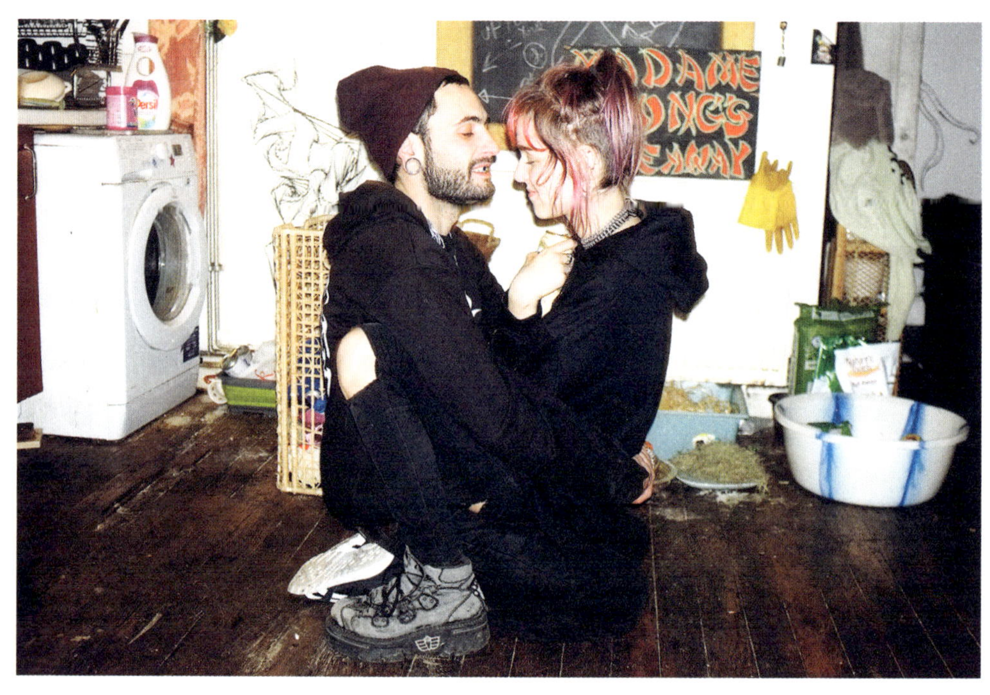

MADAME
WONG'S
TAKEAWAY

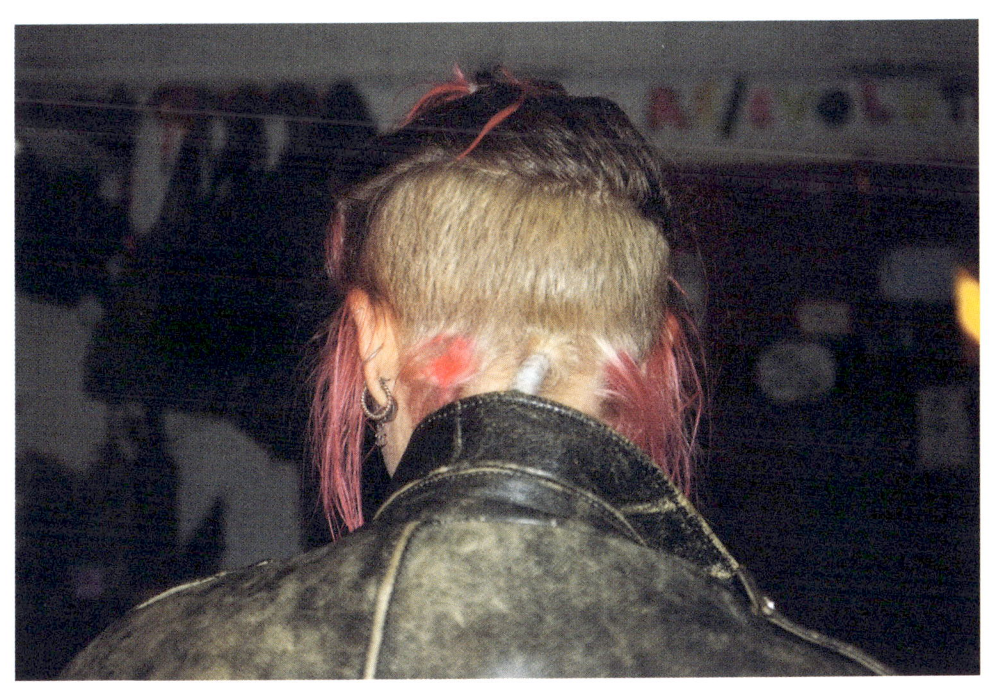

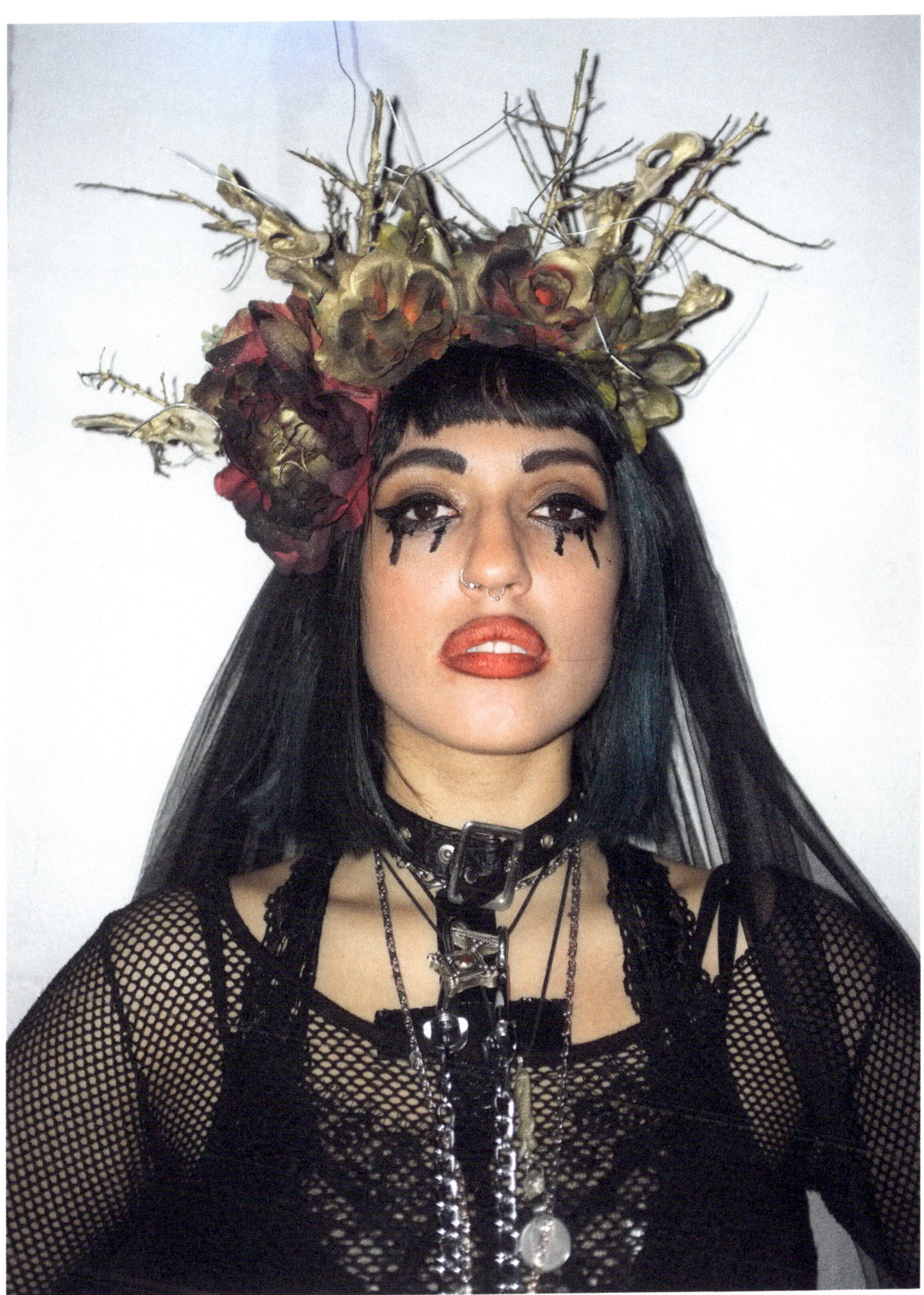

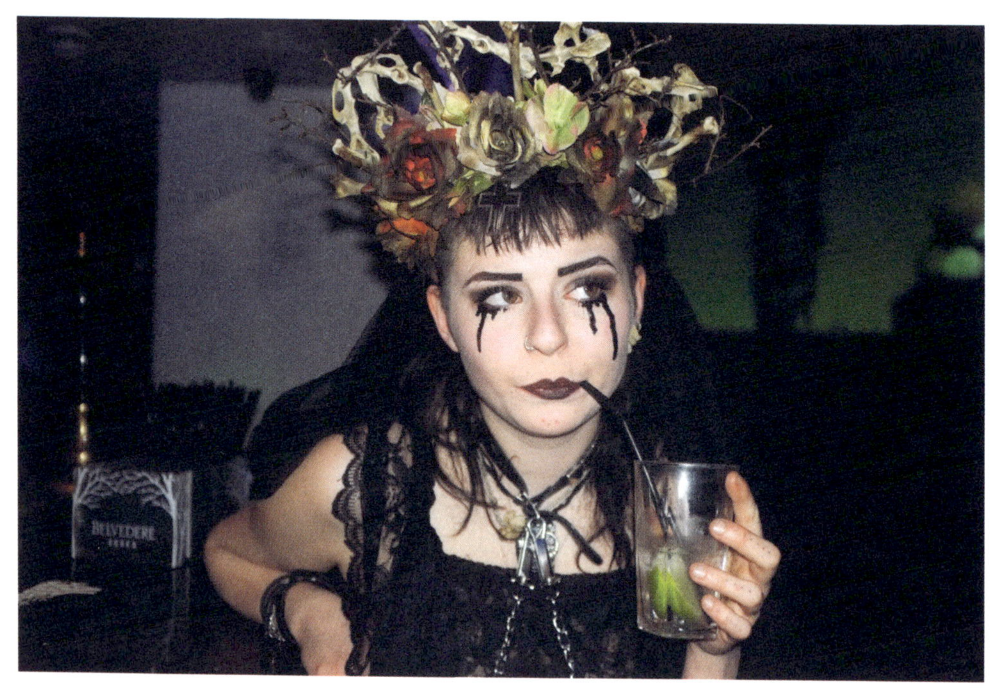

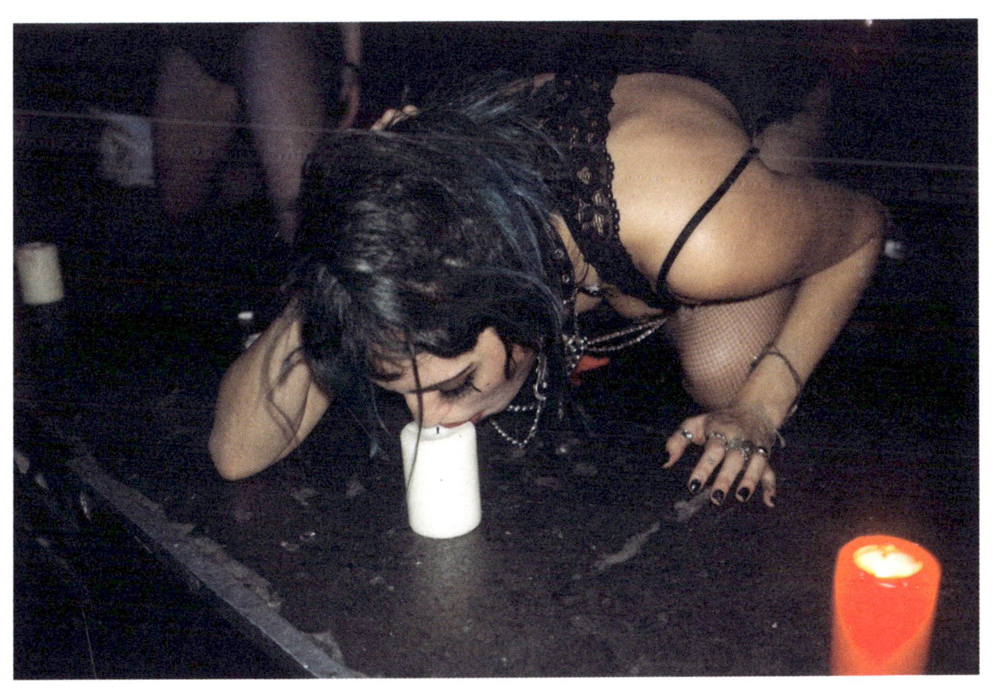

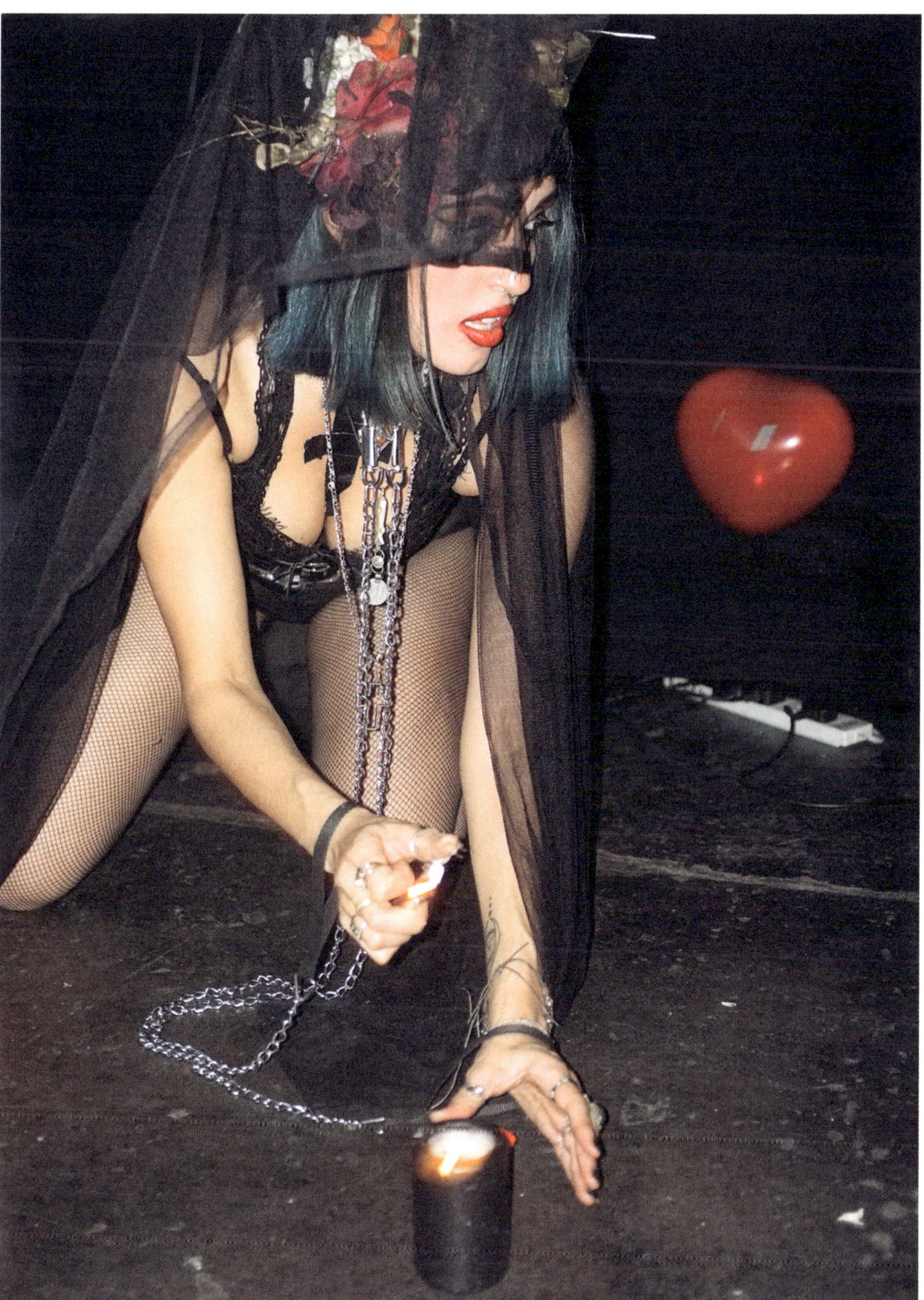

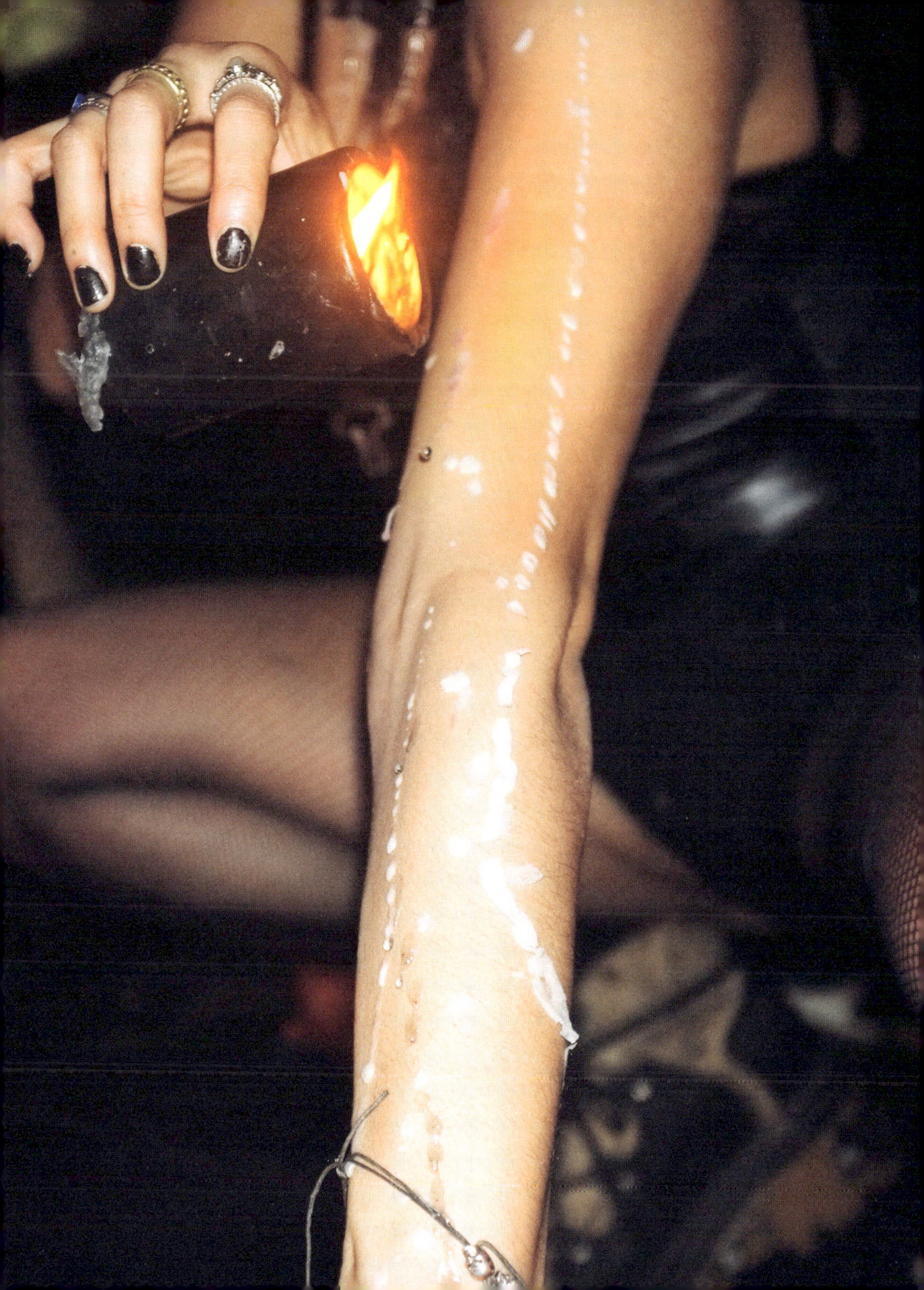

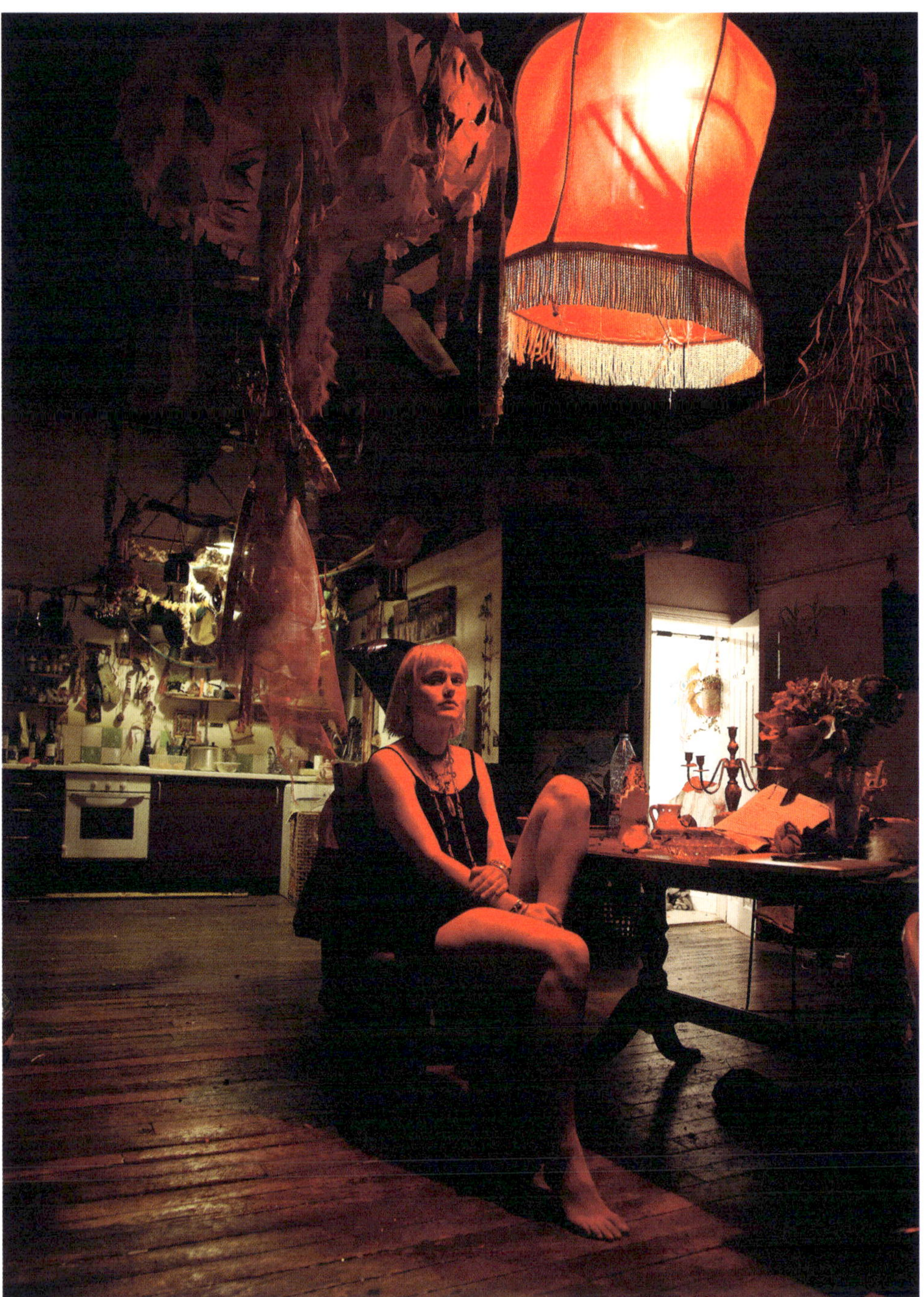

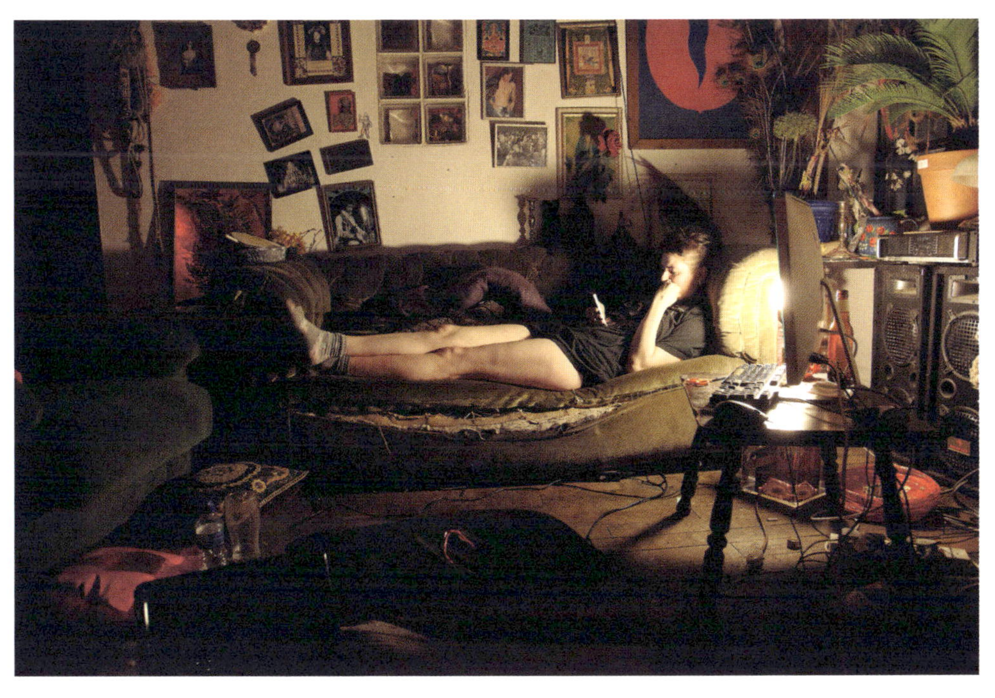

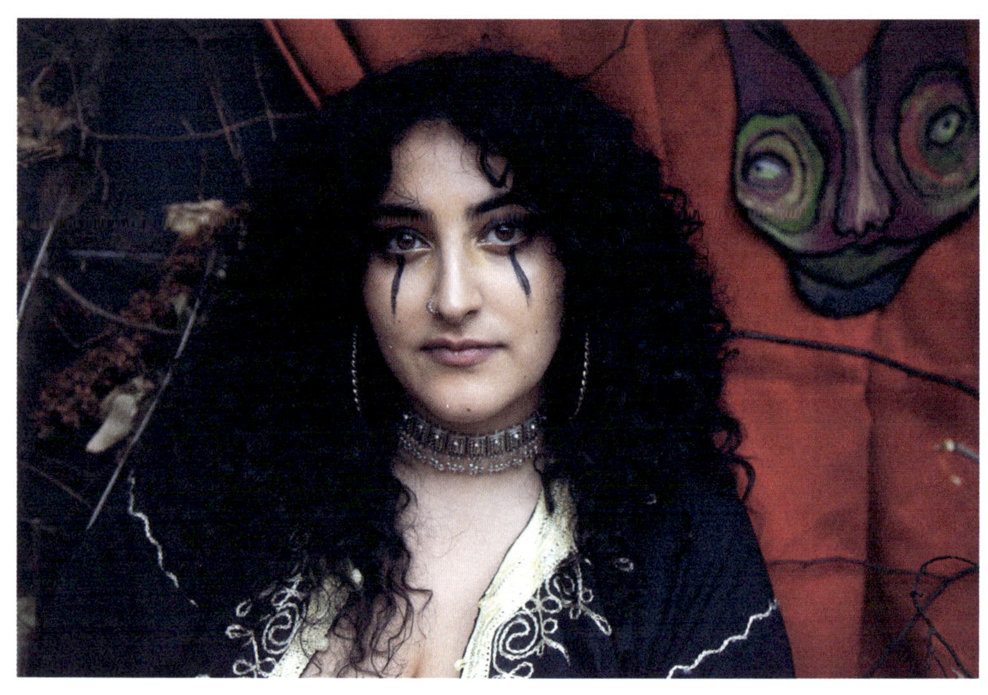

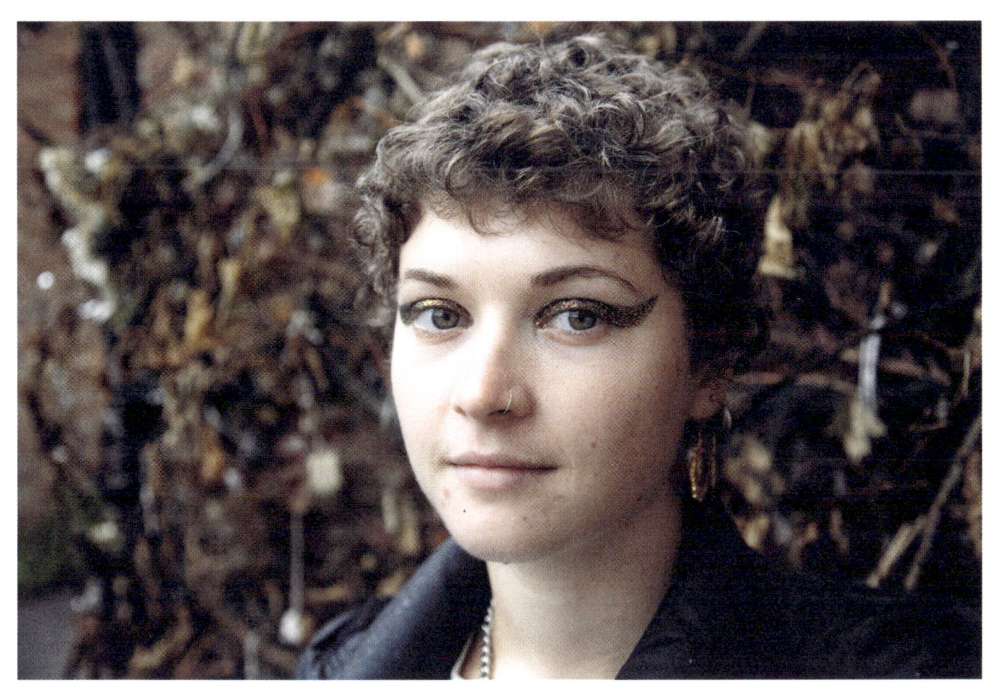

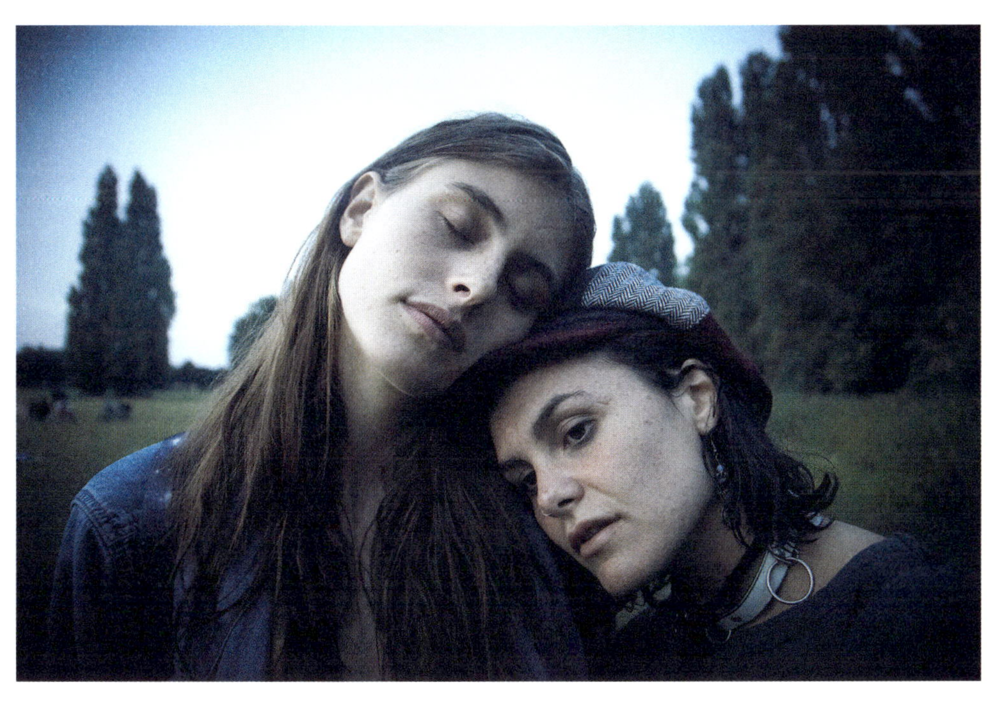

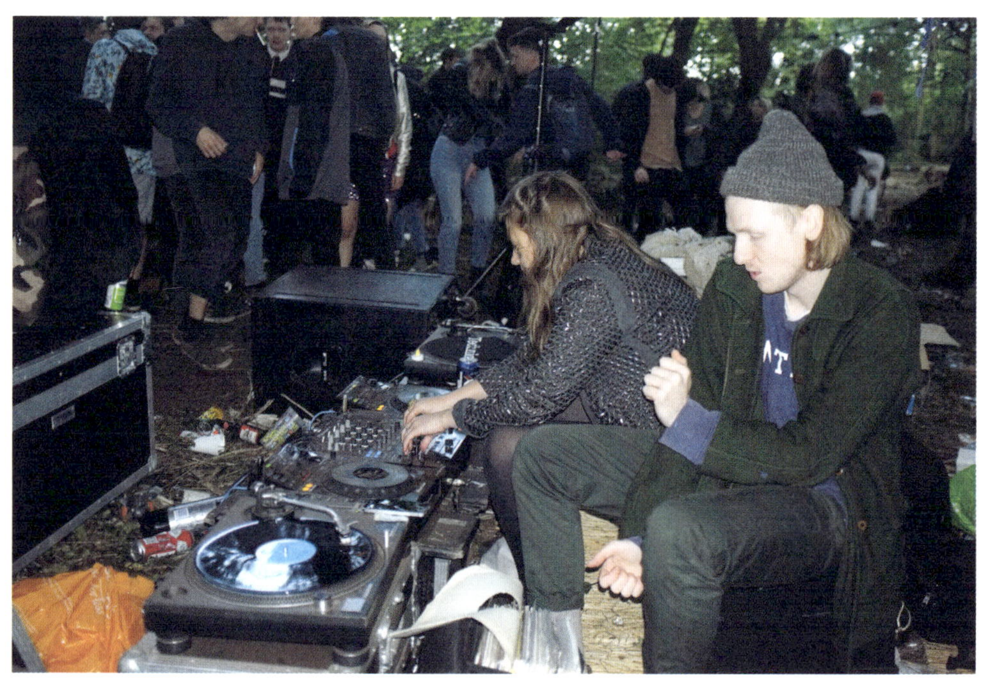

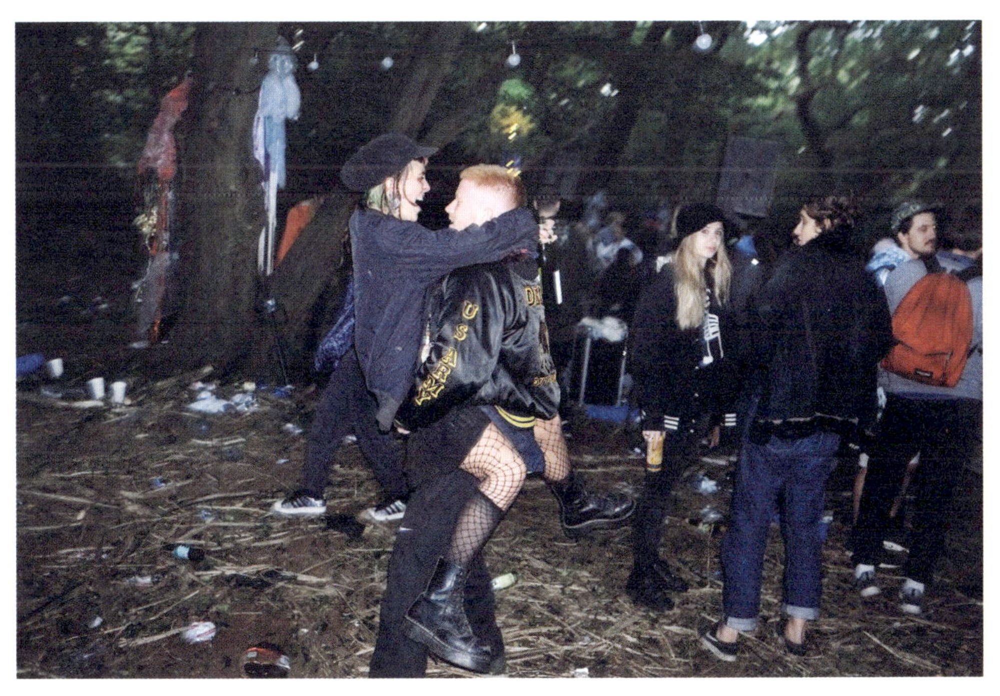

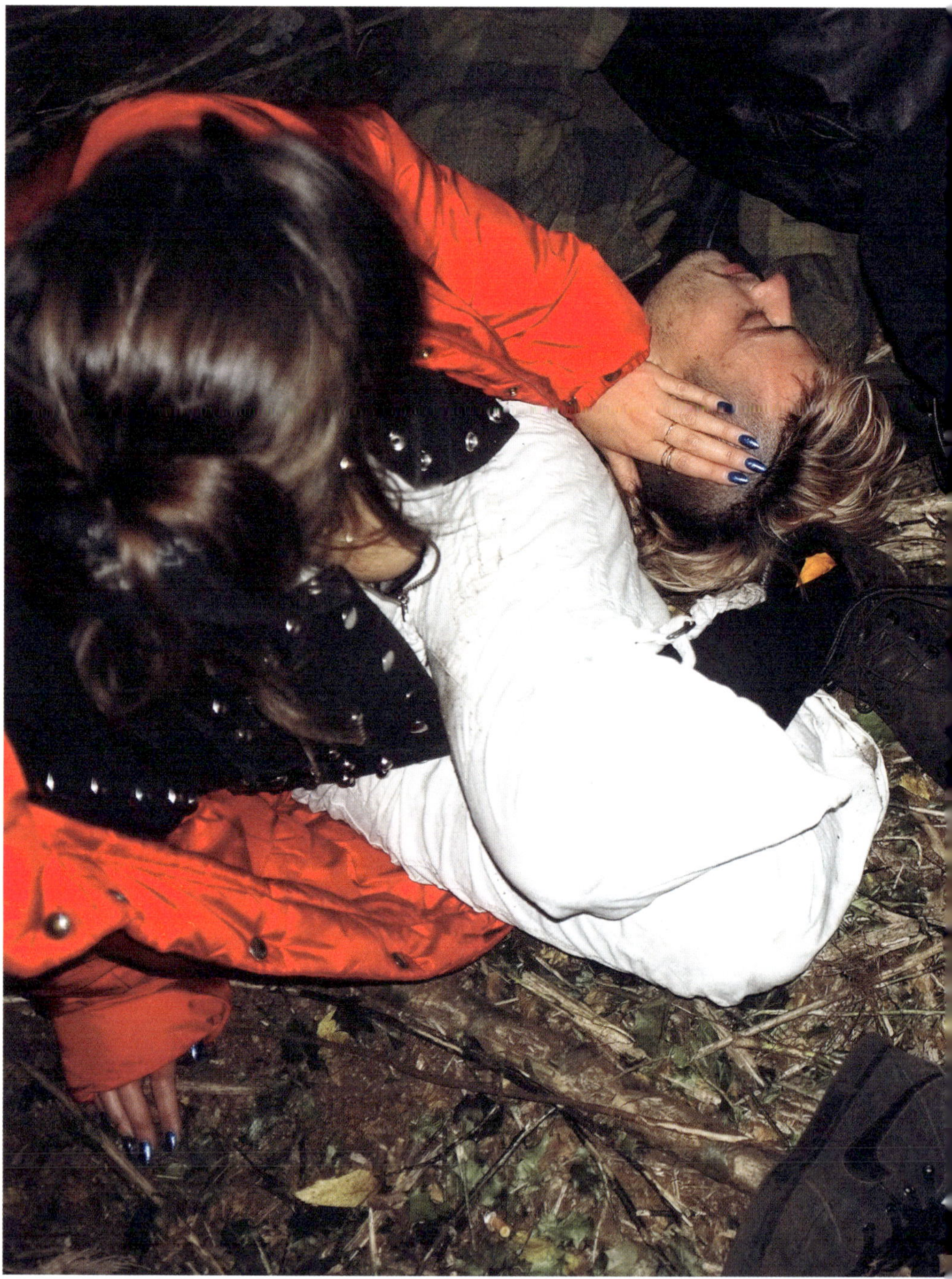

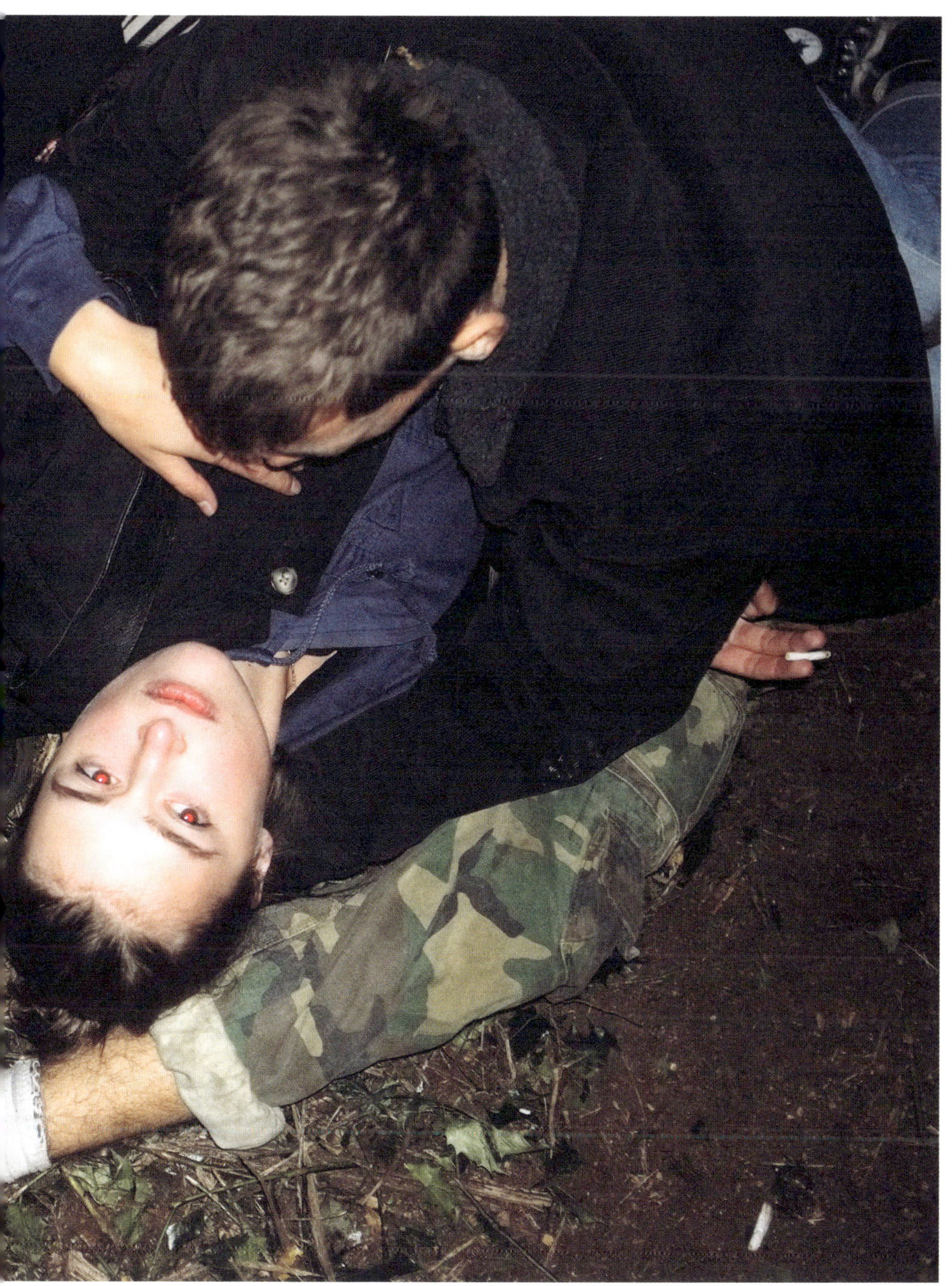

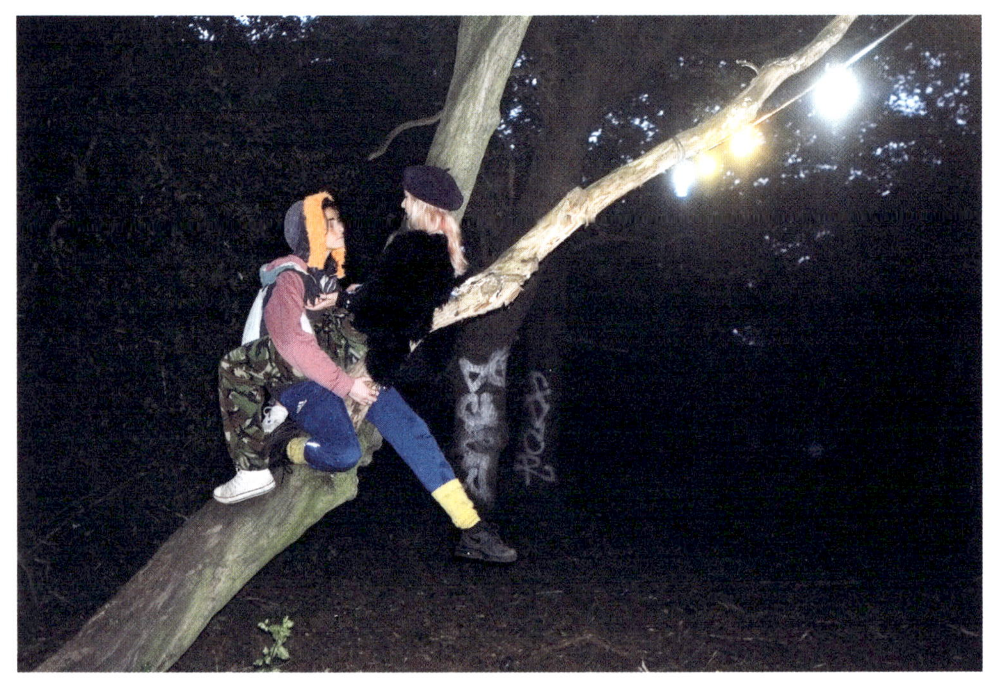

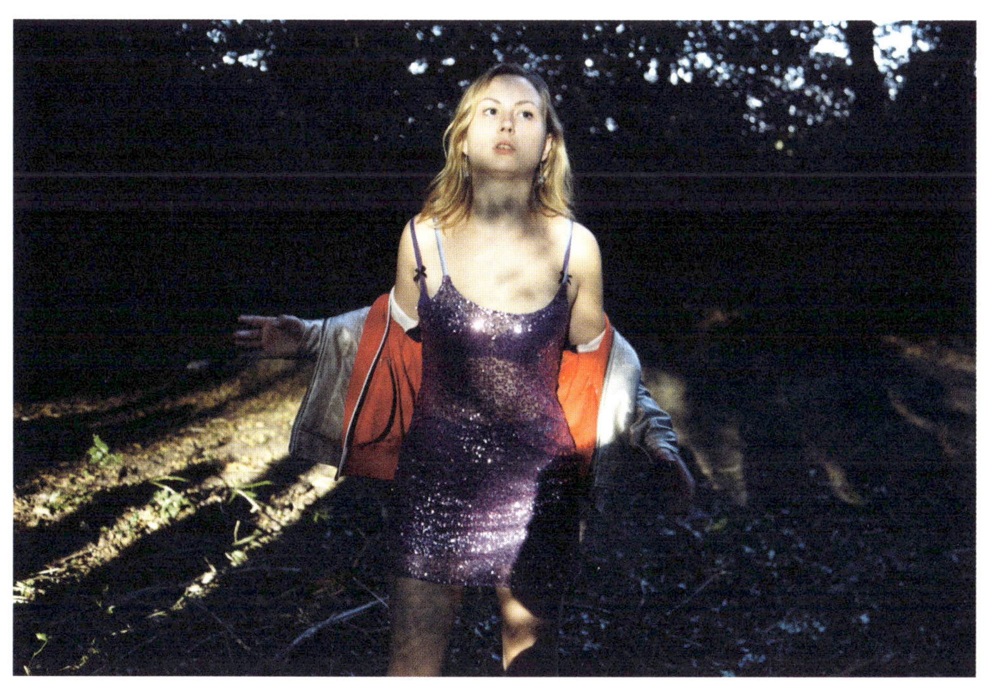

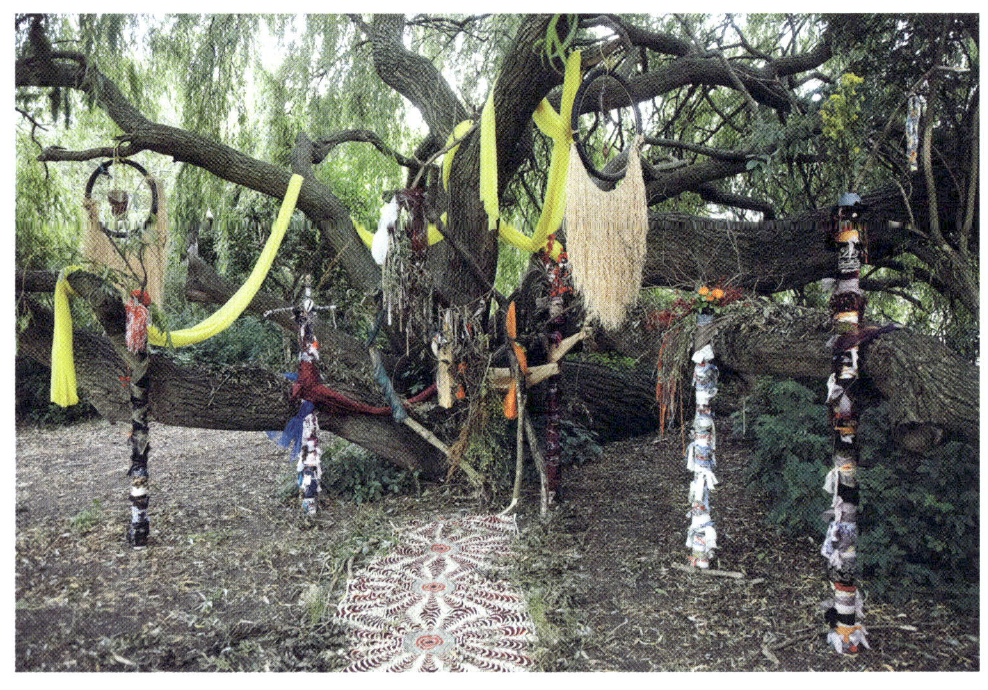

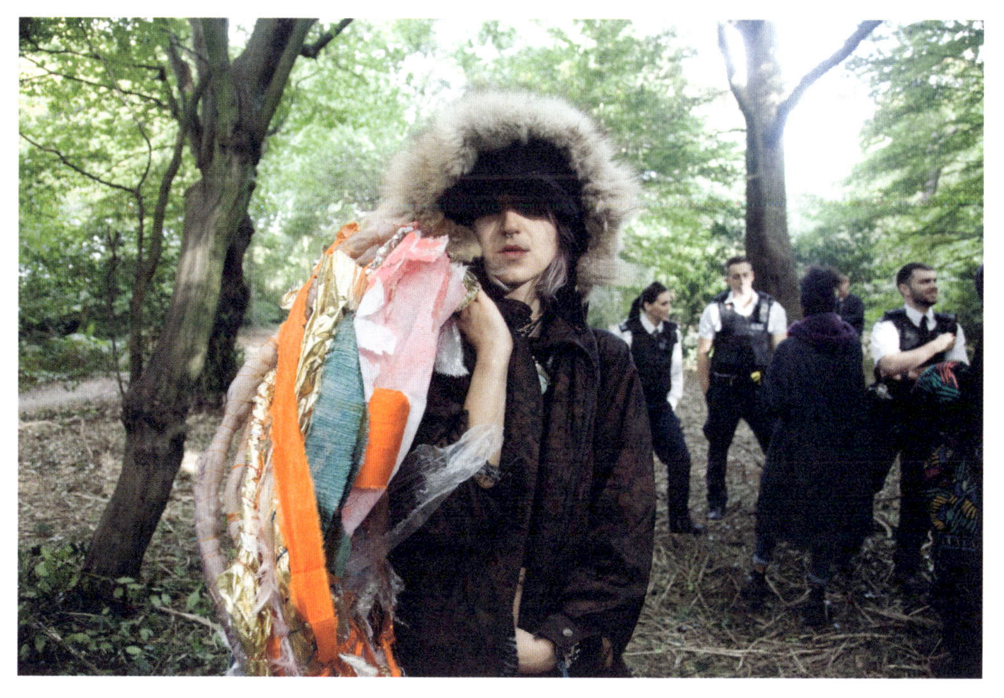

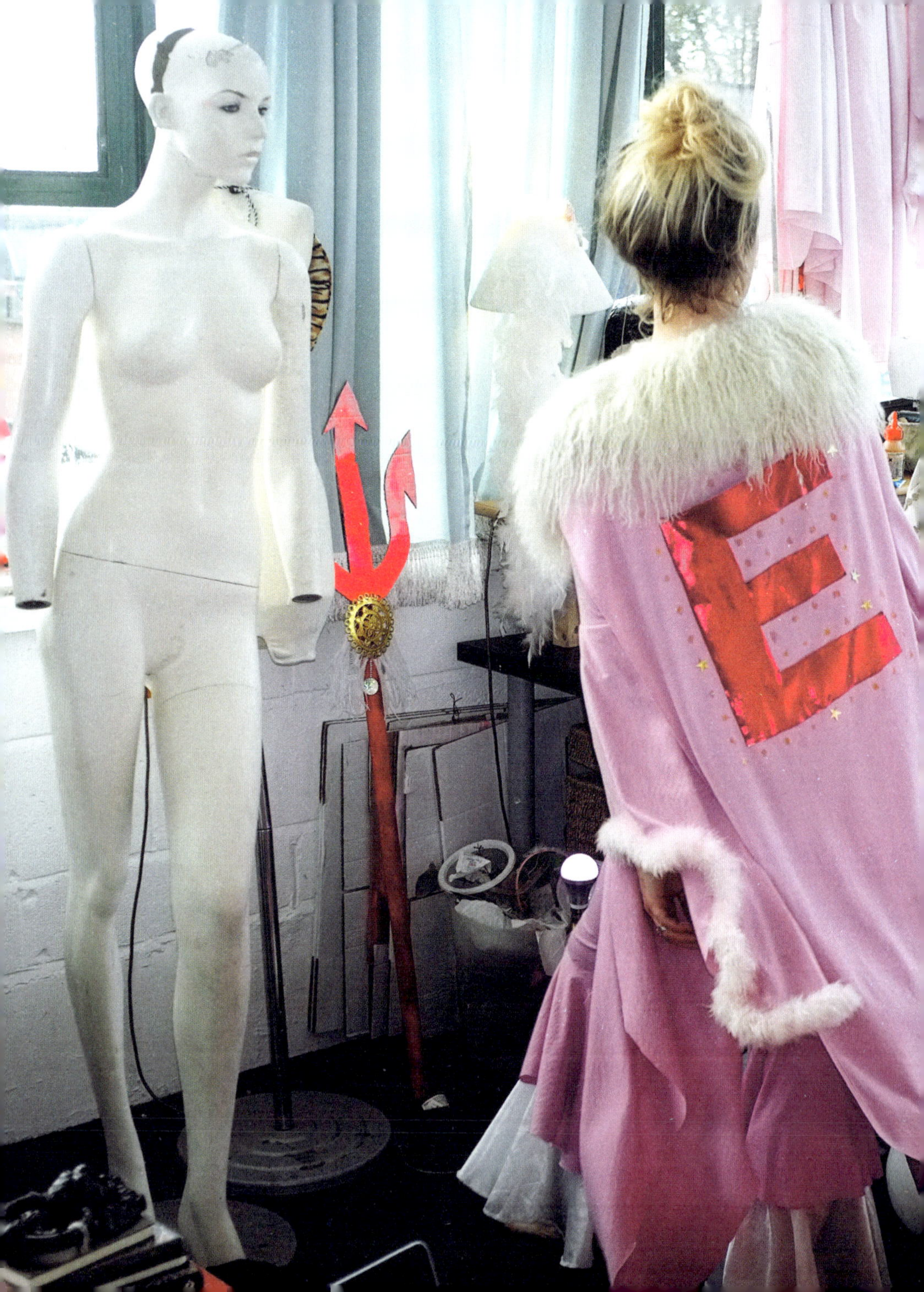

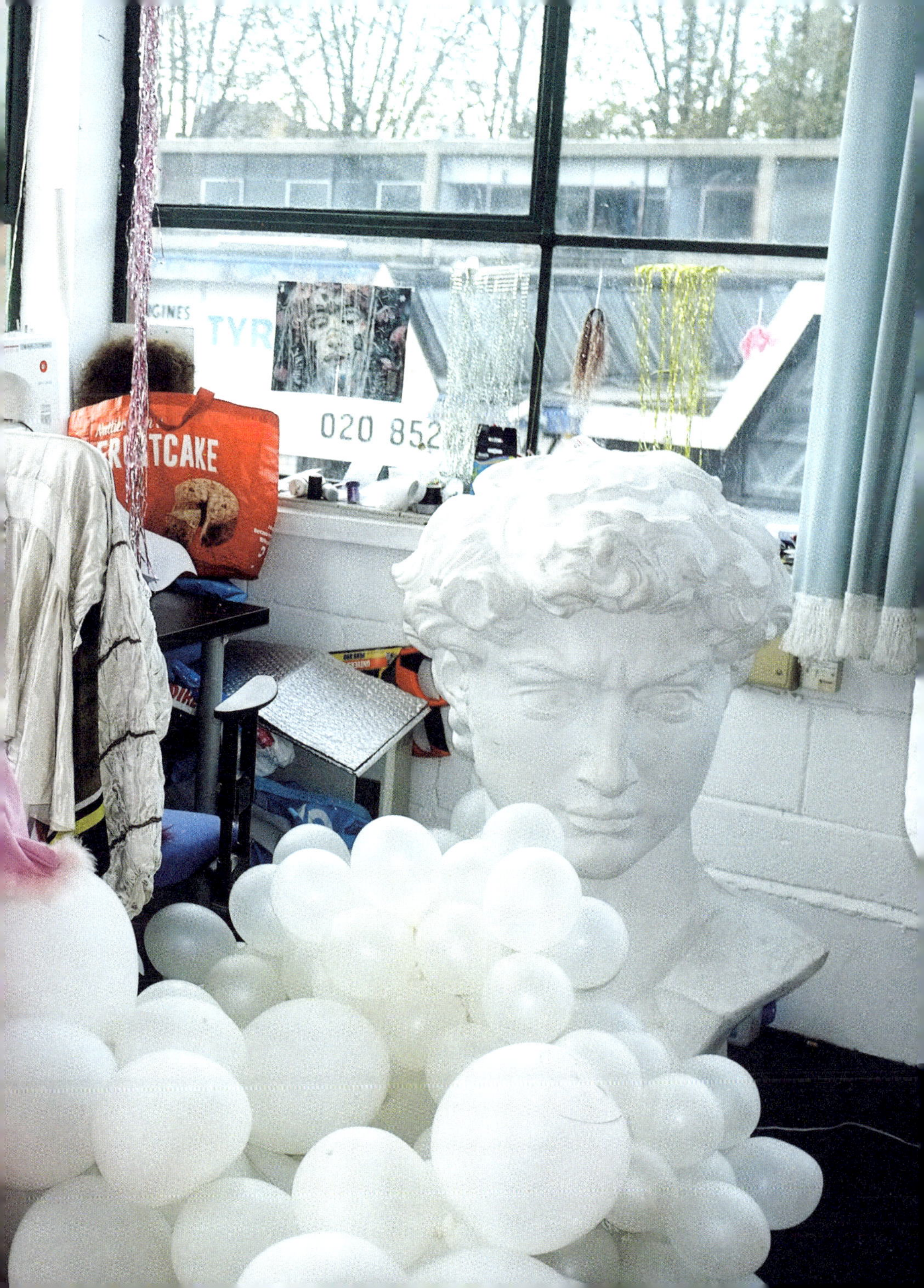
FRUITCAKE
GINES
TYR
020 852

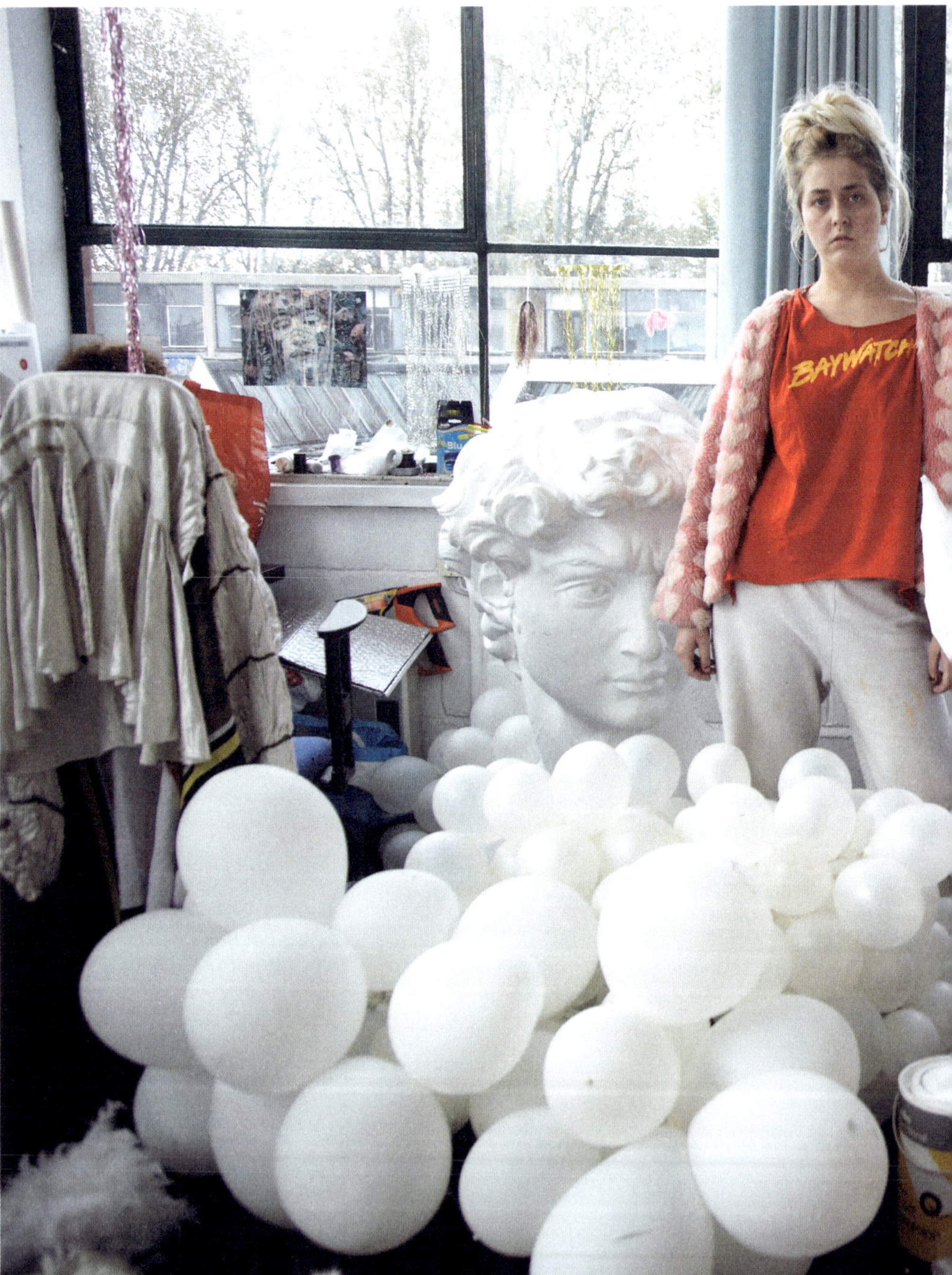
BAYWATCH

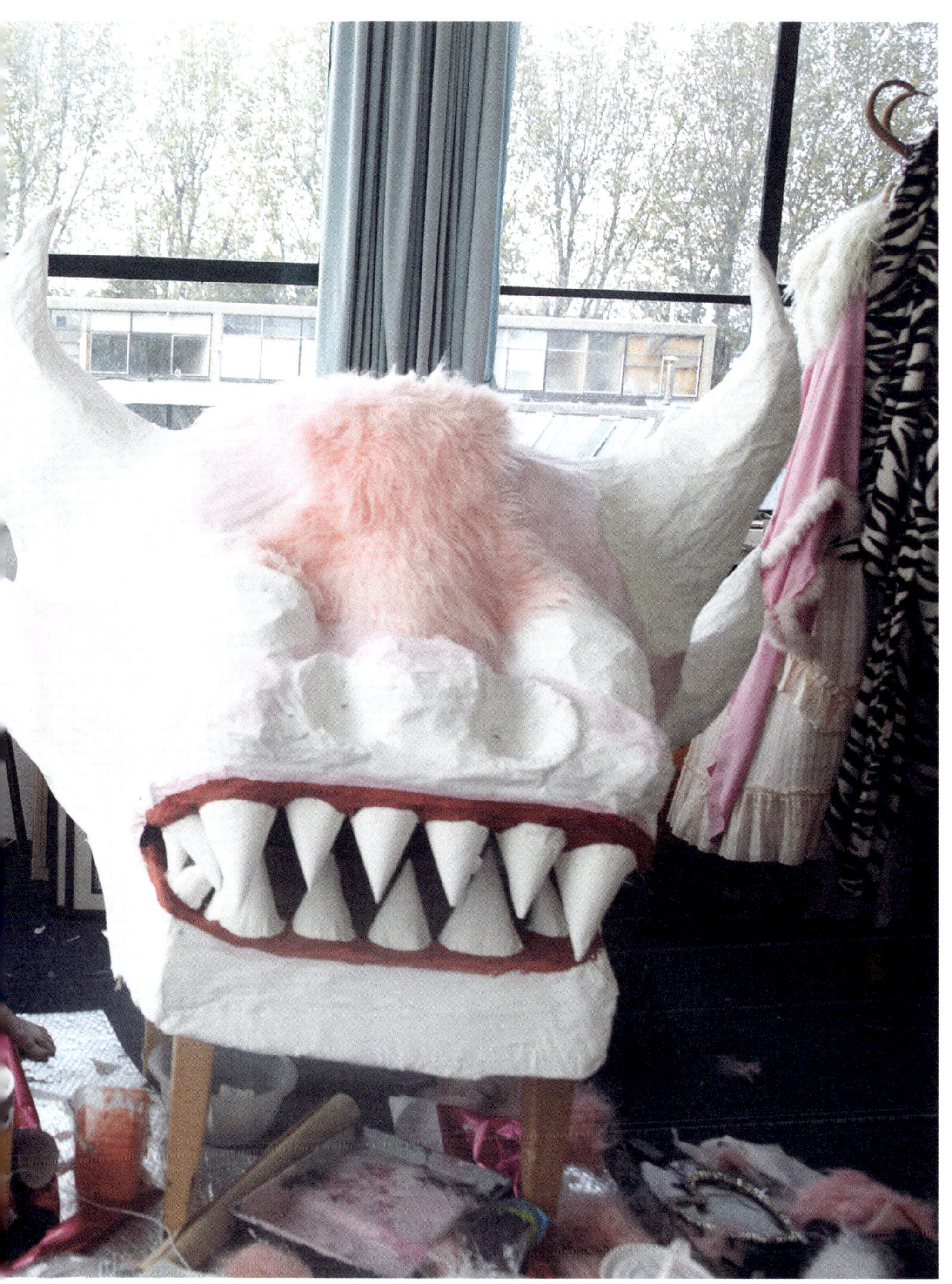

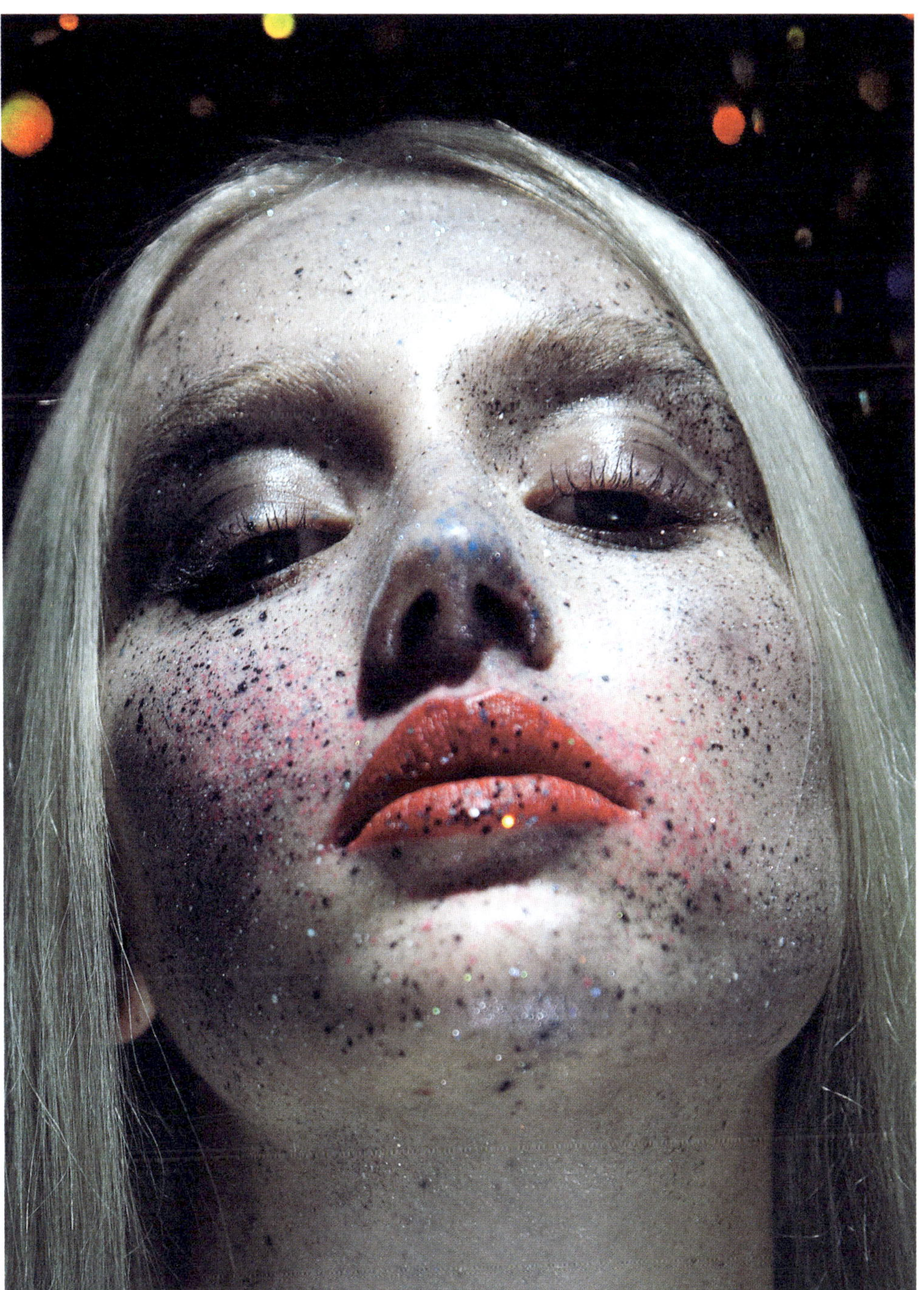

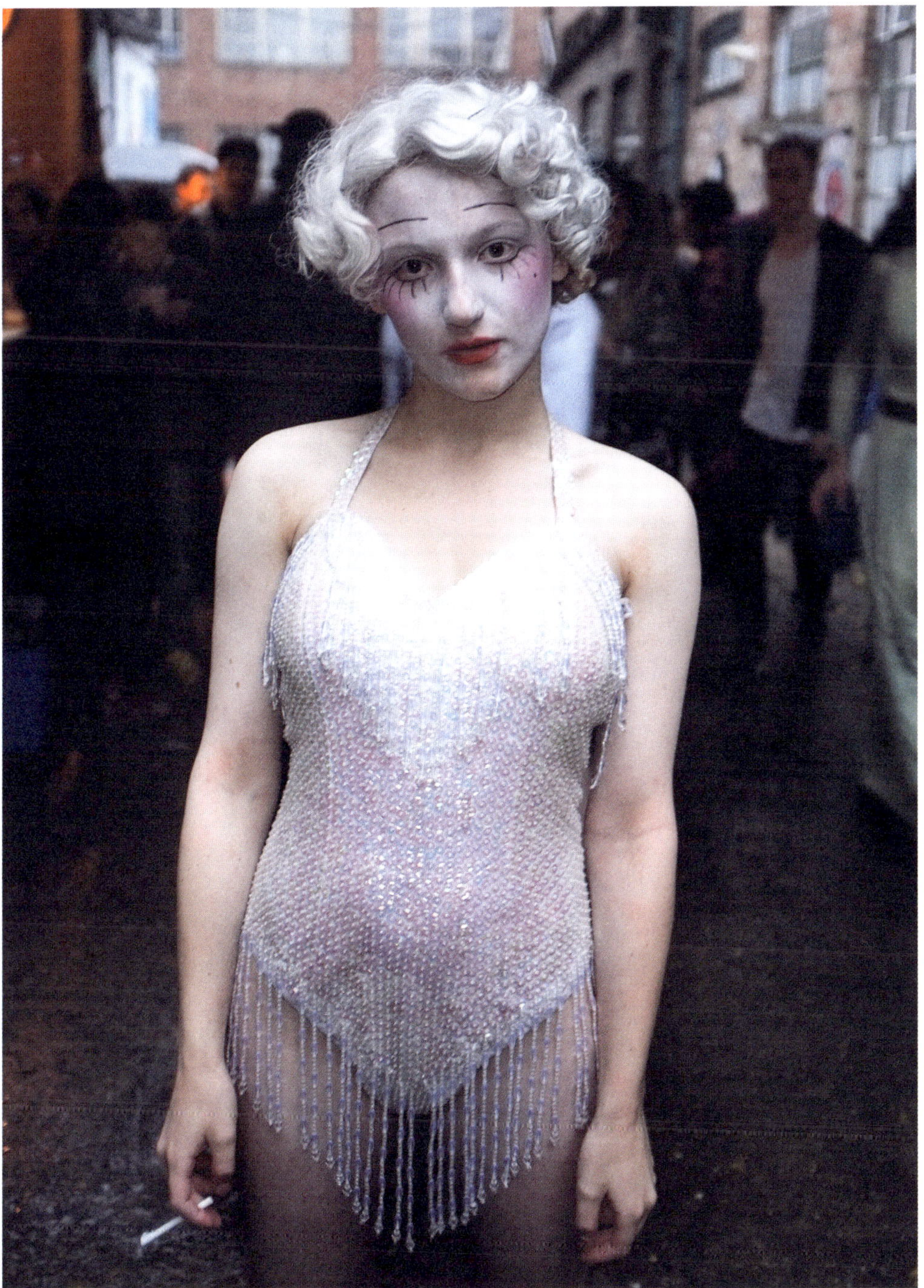

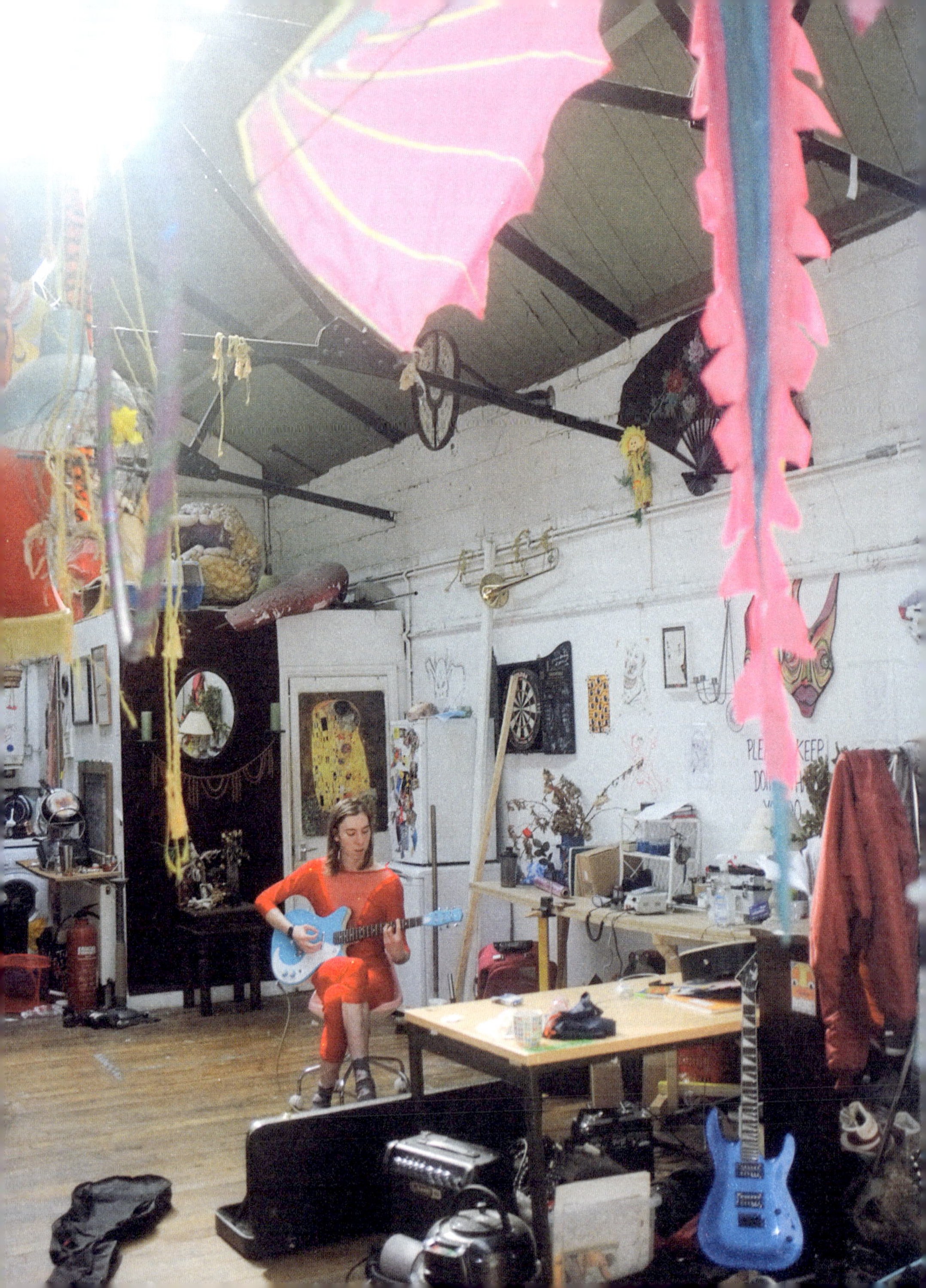

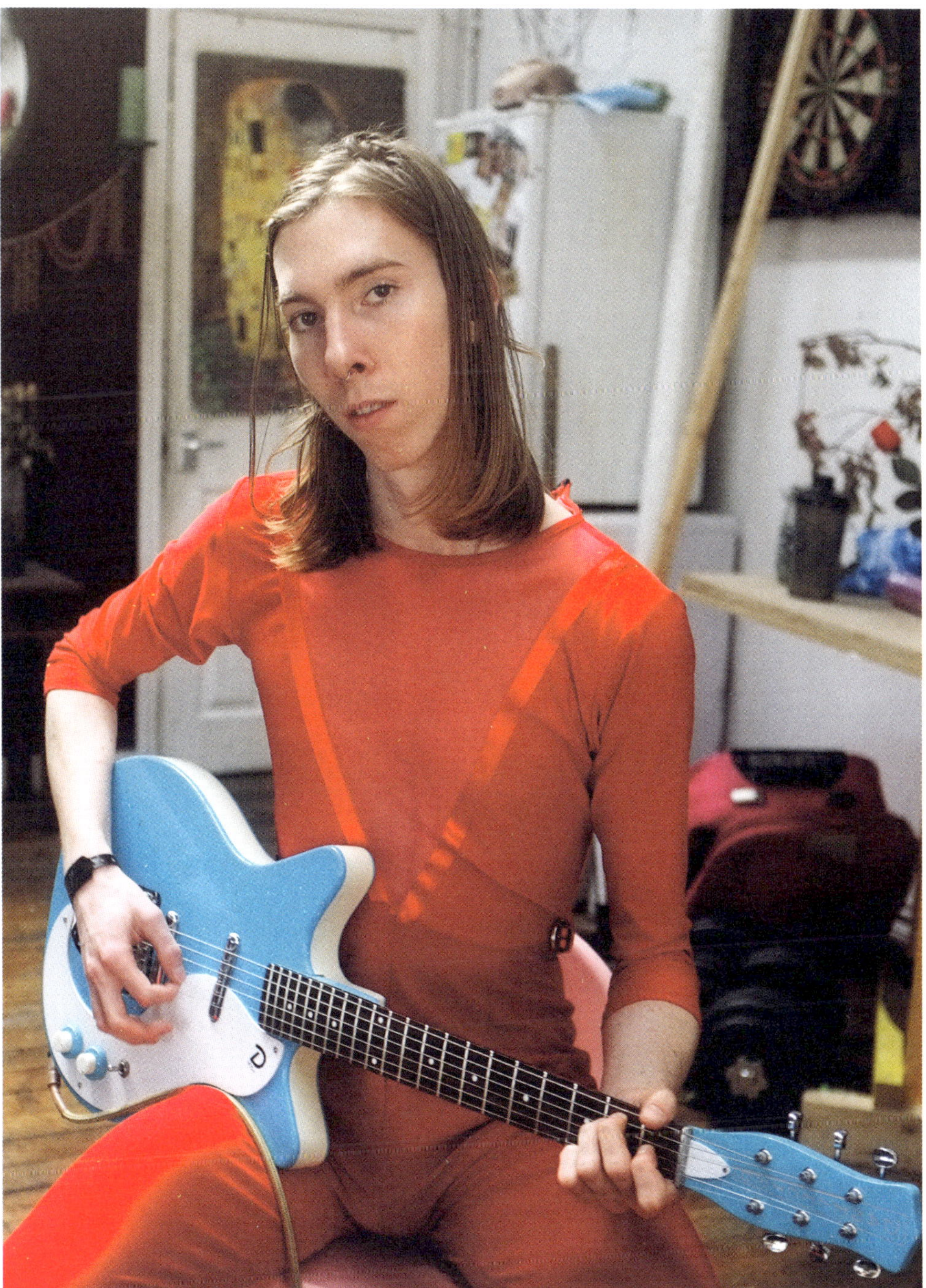

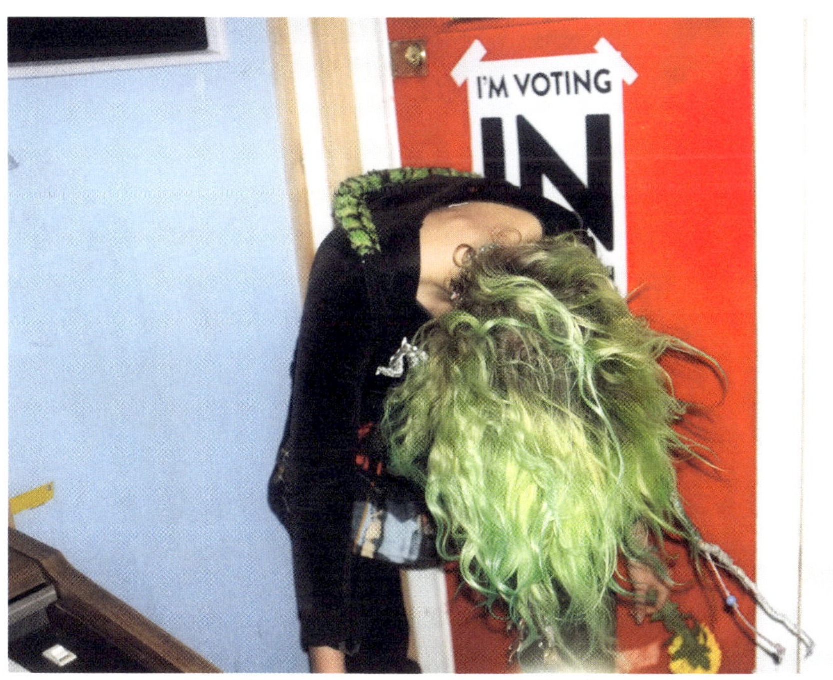
I'M VOTING
IN

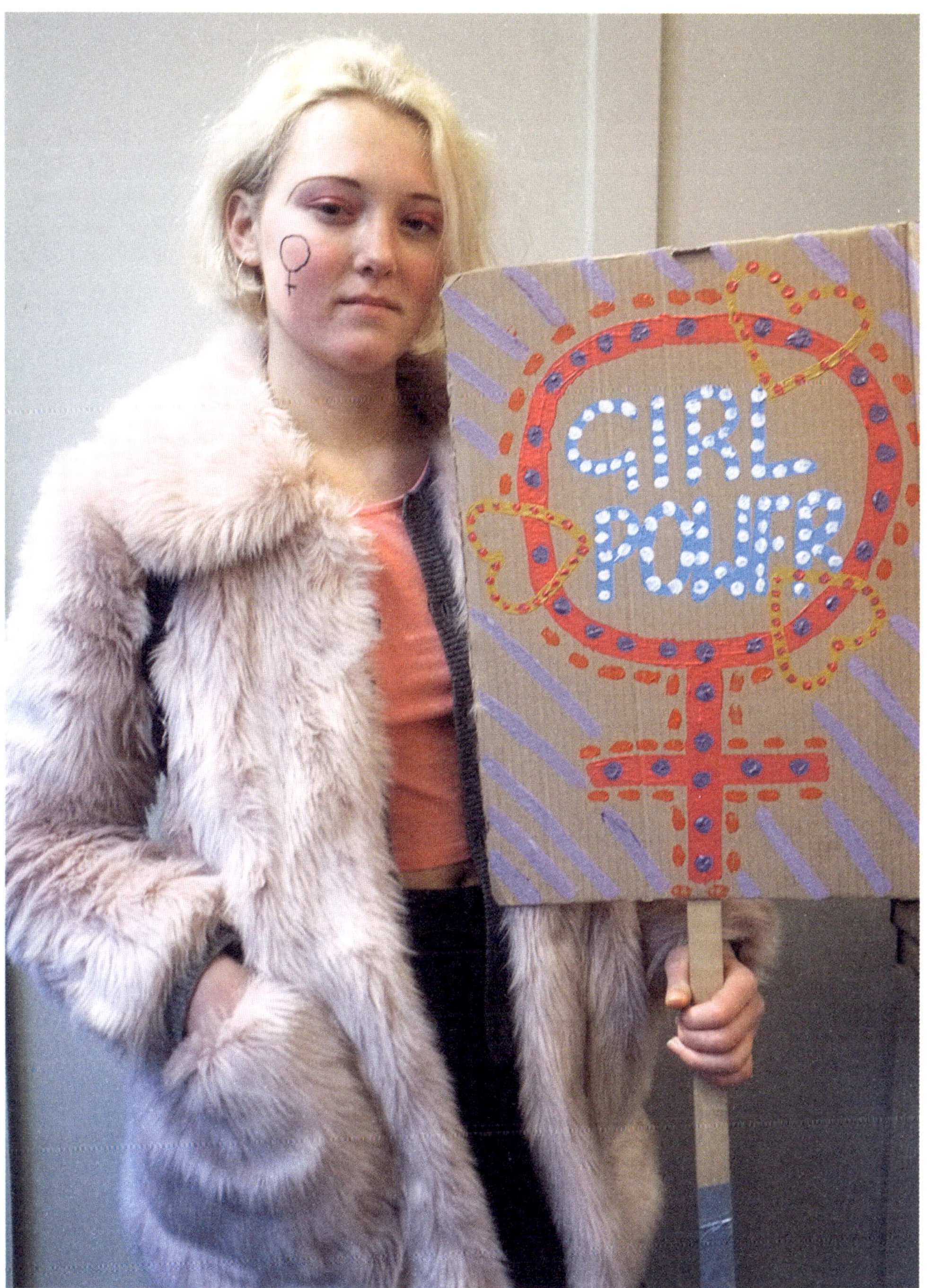

GIRL
POWER

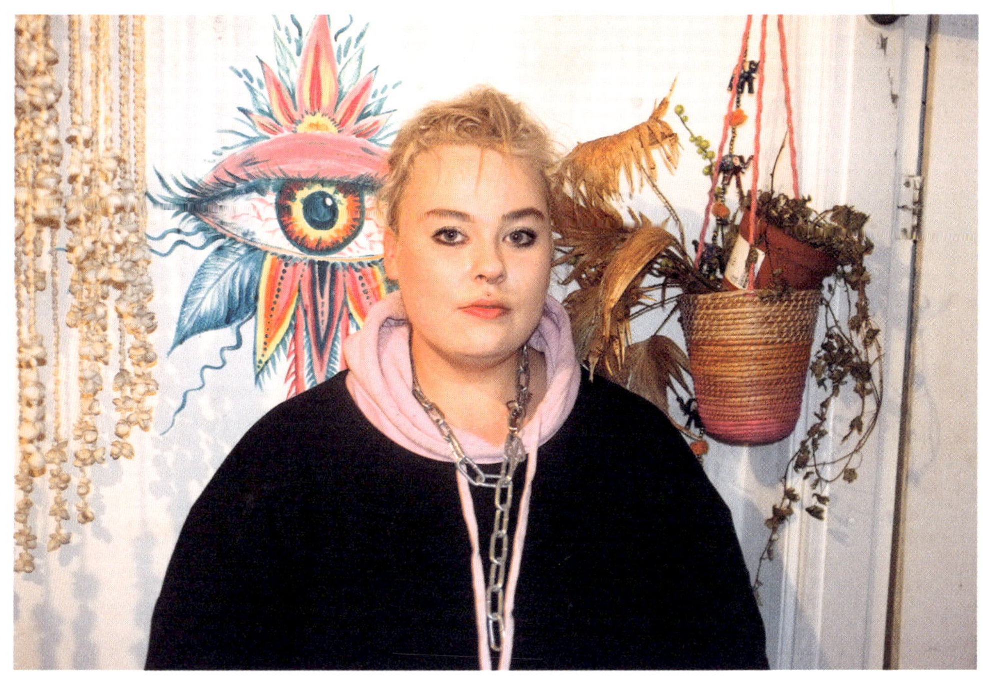

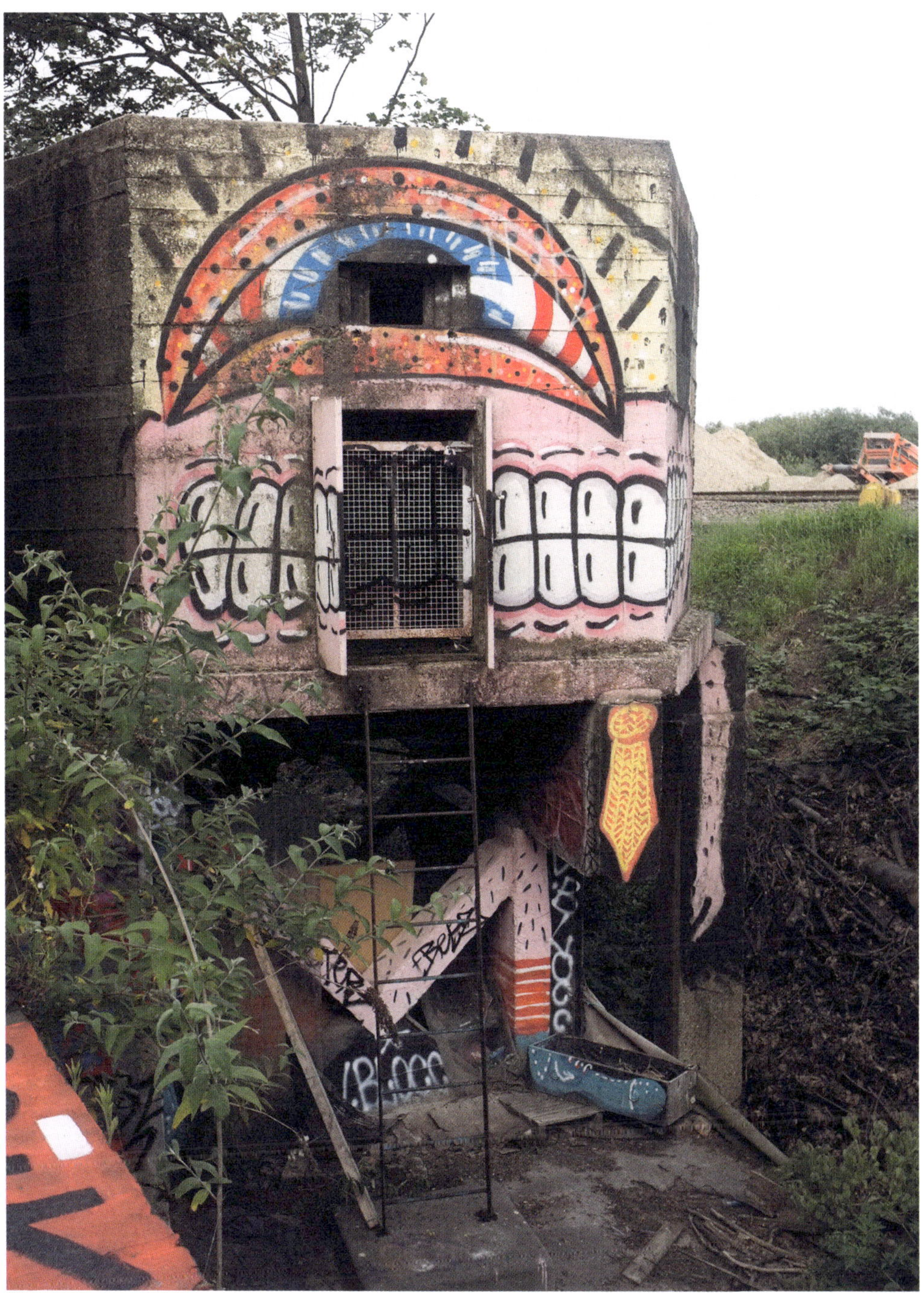

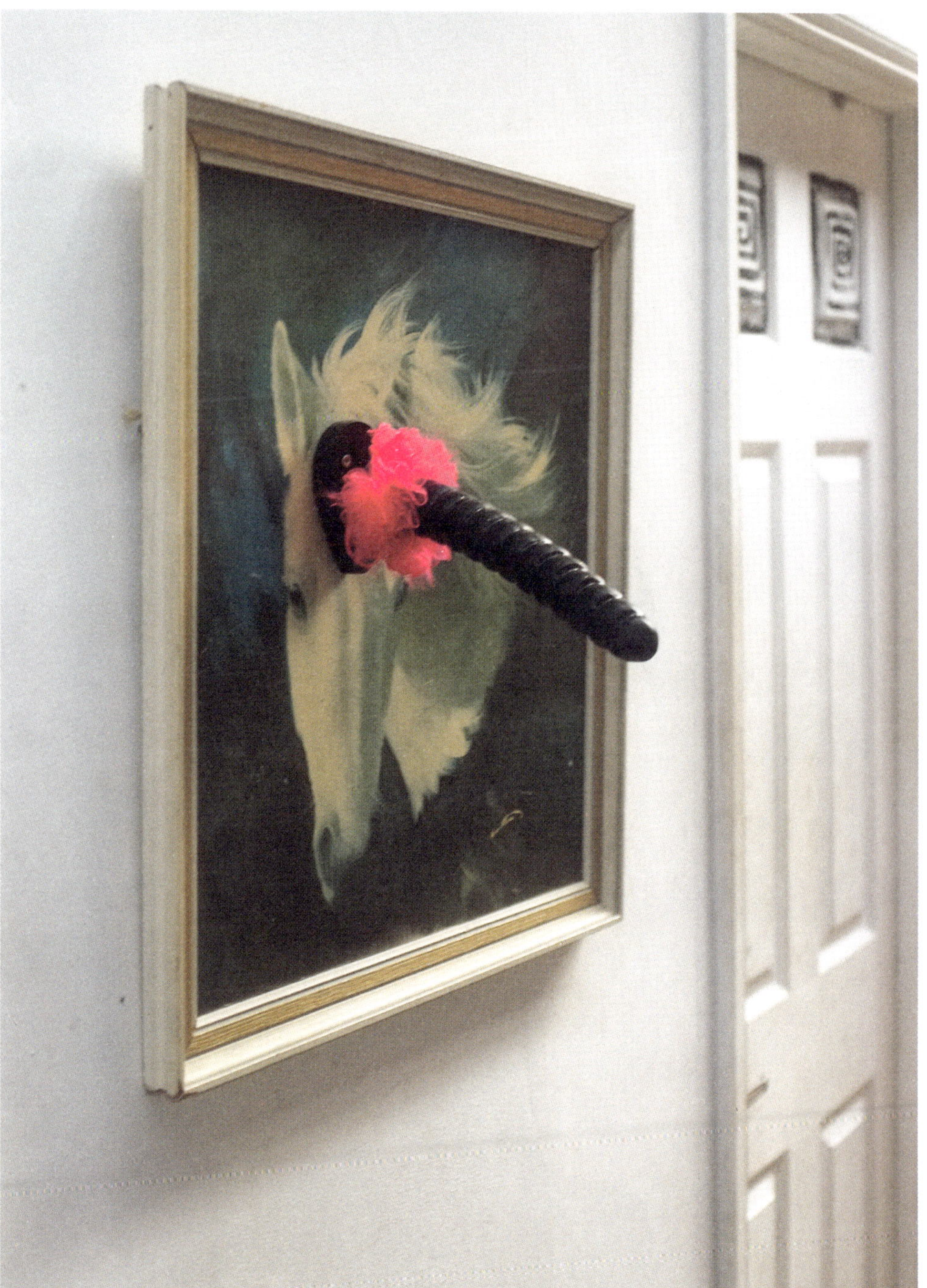

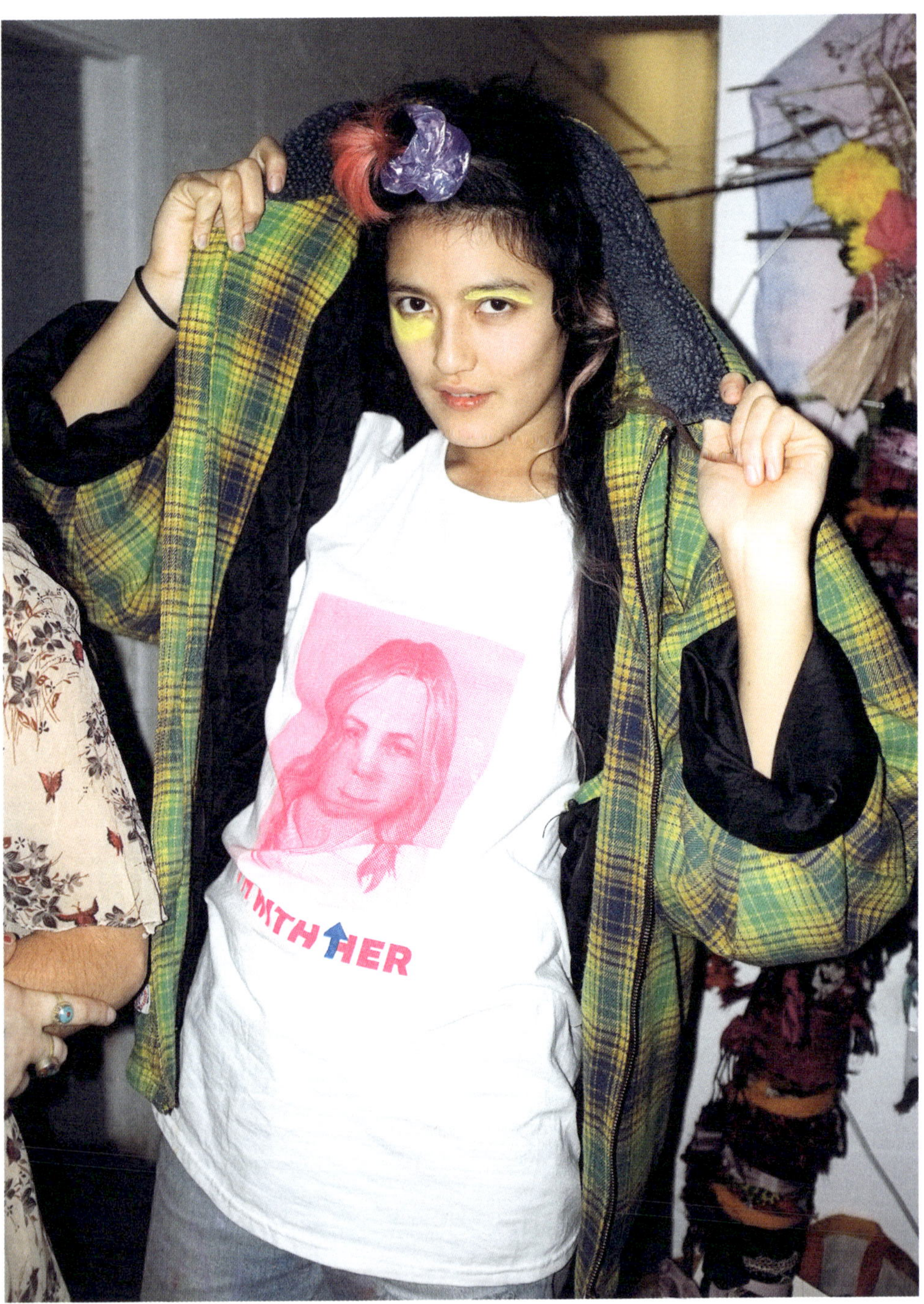
I'M WITH HER

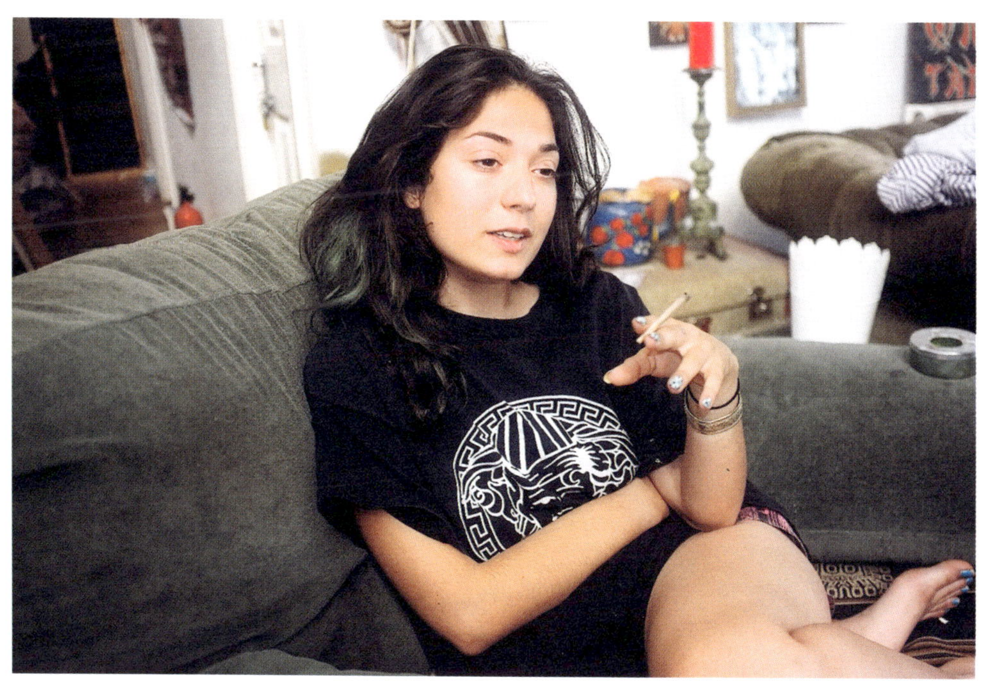

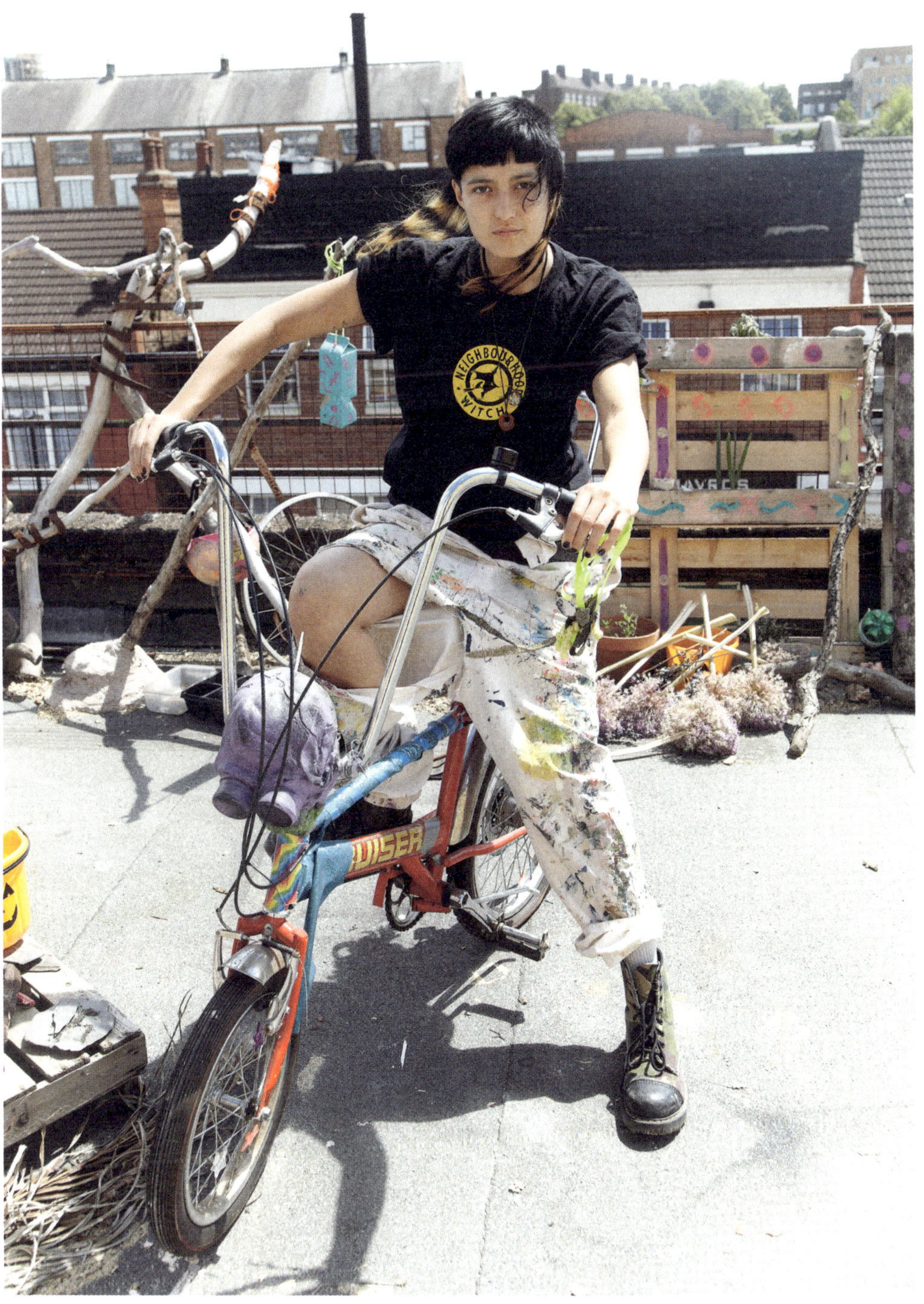

NEIGHBOURHOOD
WITCH
WISER

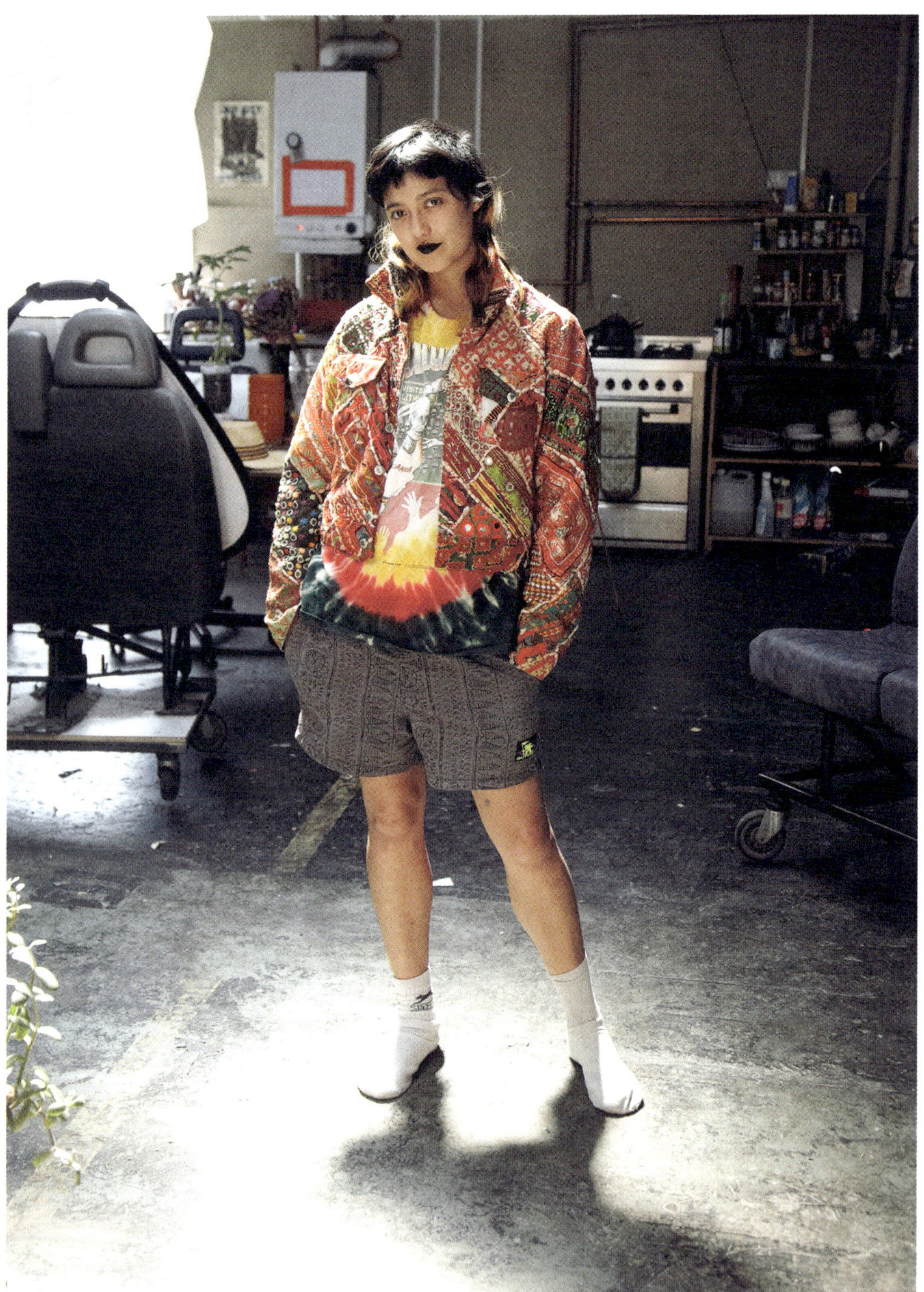

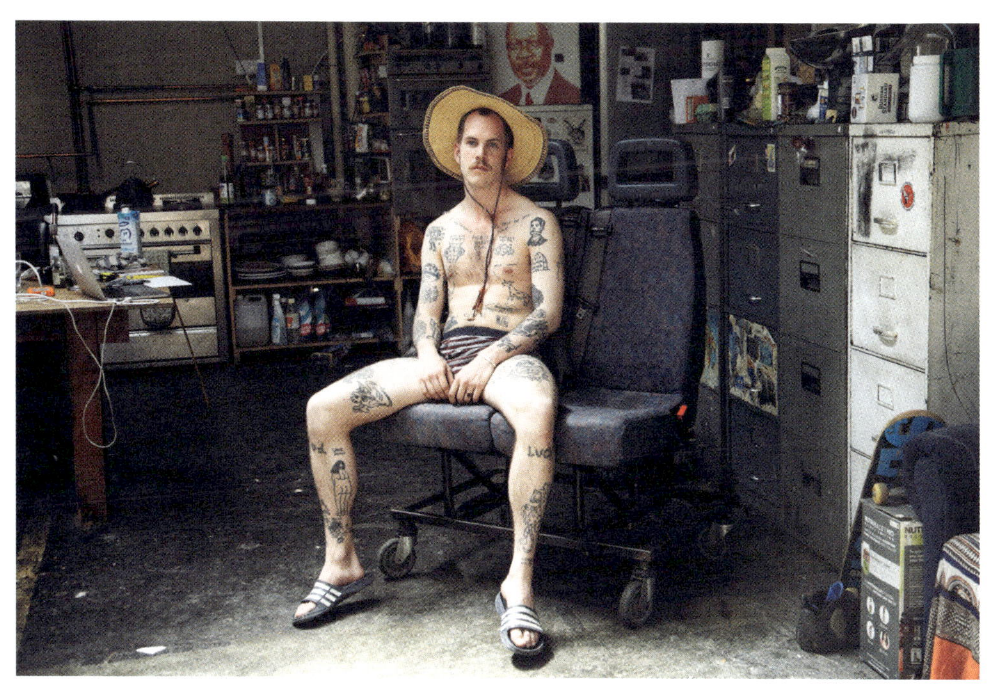

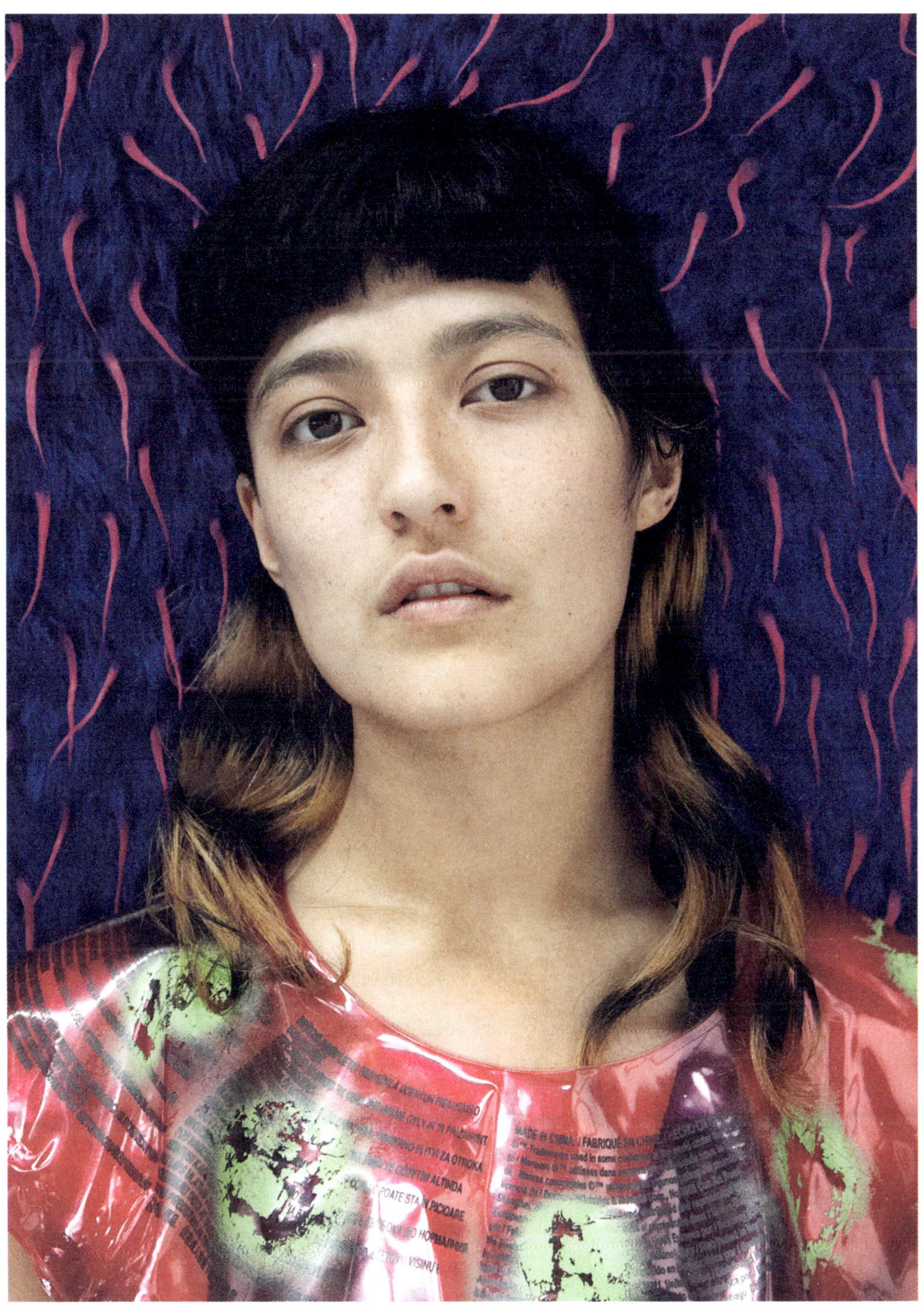

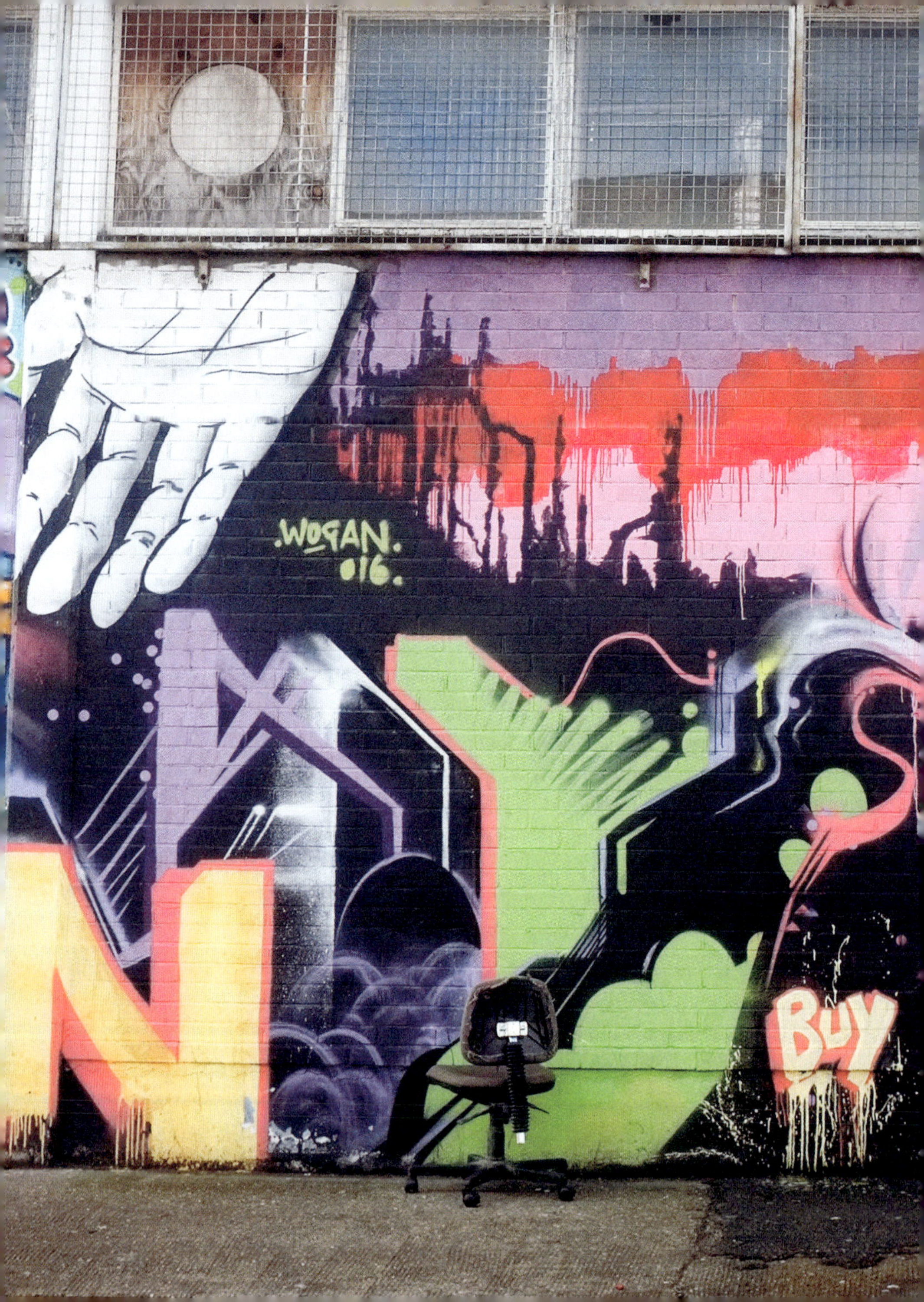

.WOGAN.
.016.
BUY

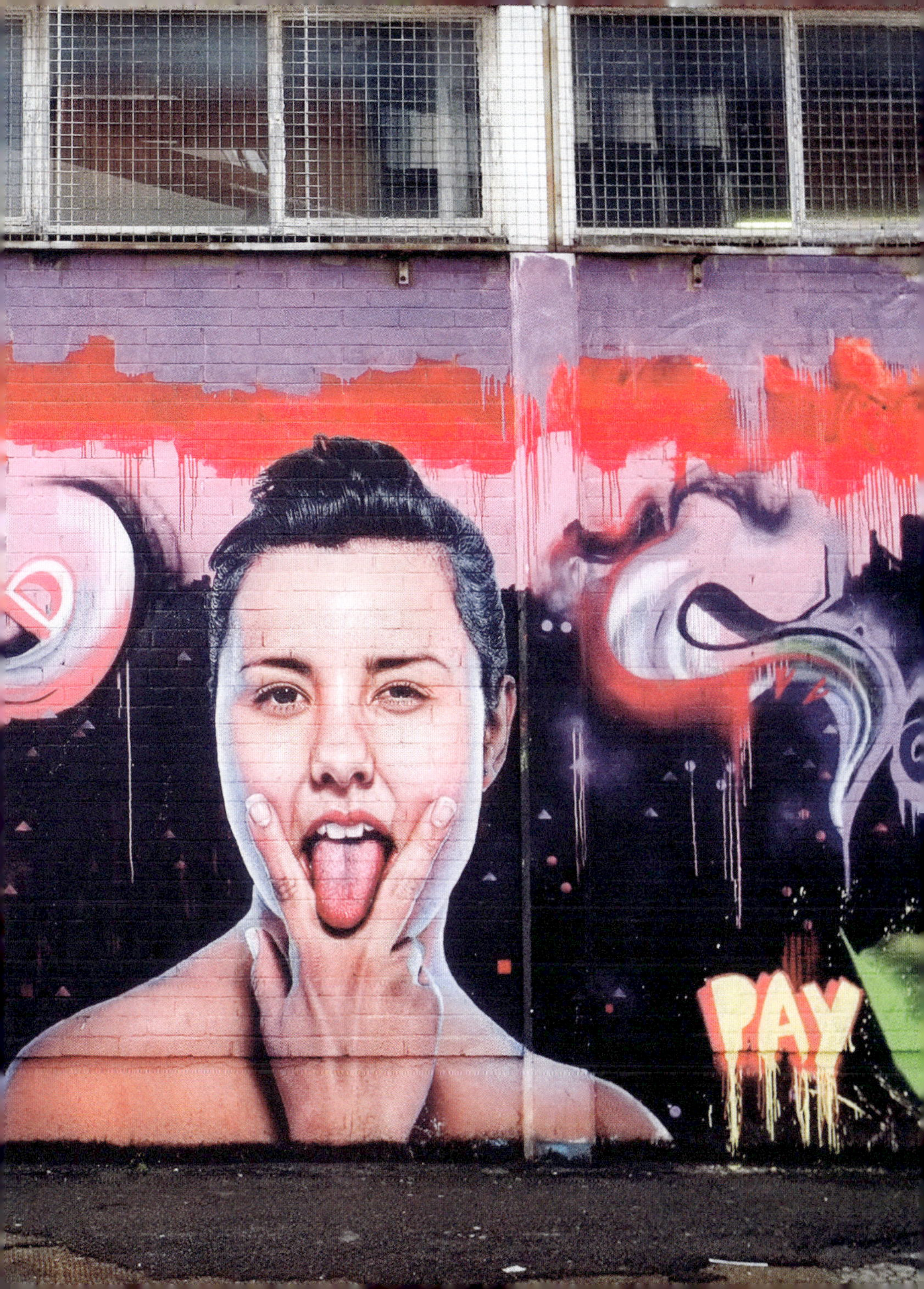

PAY

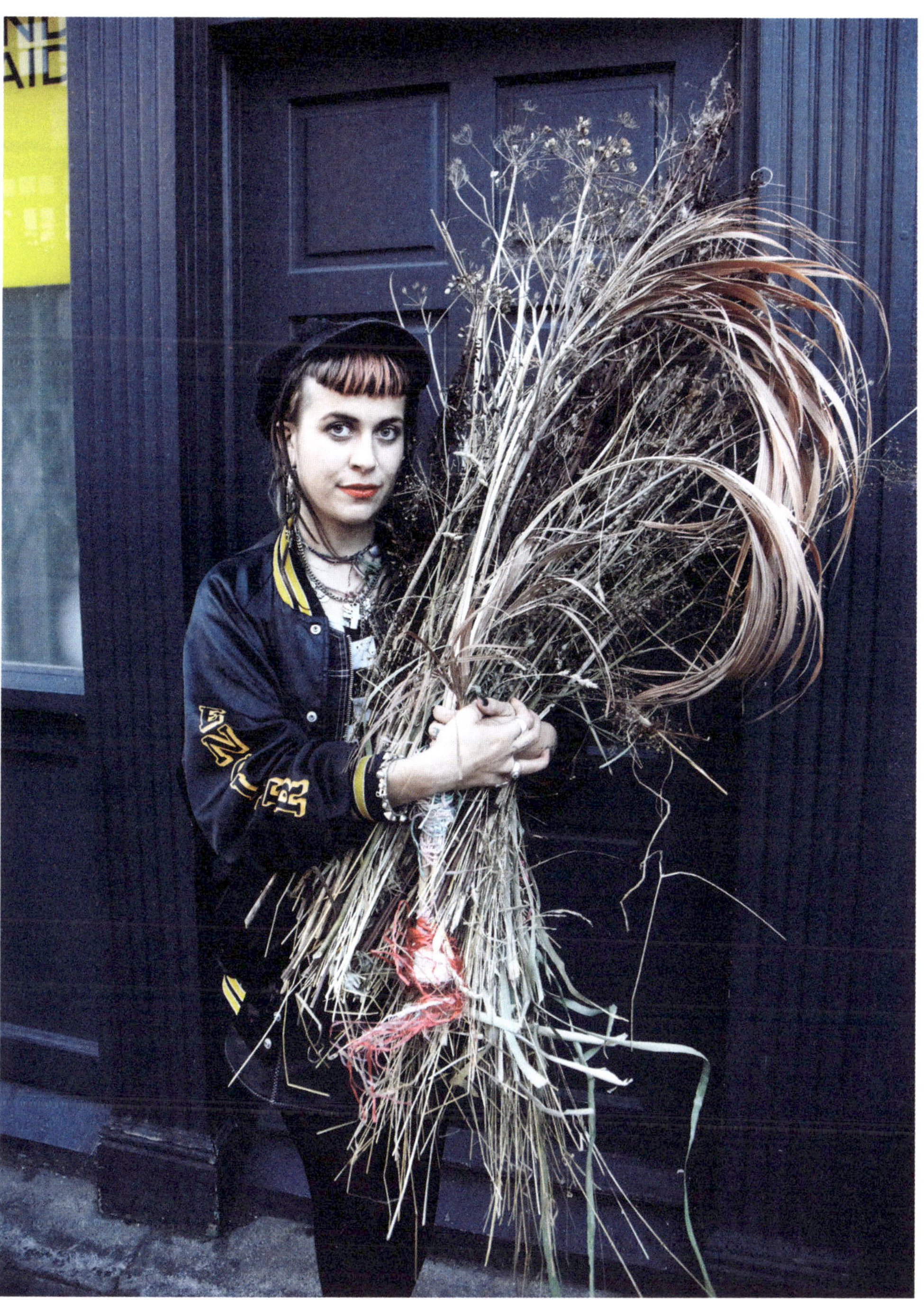

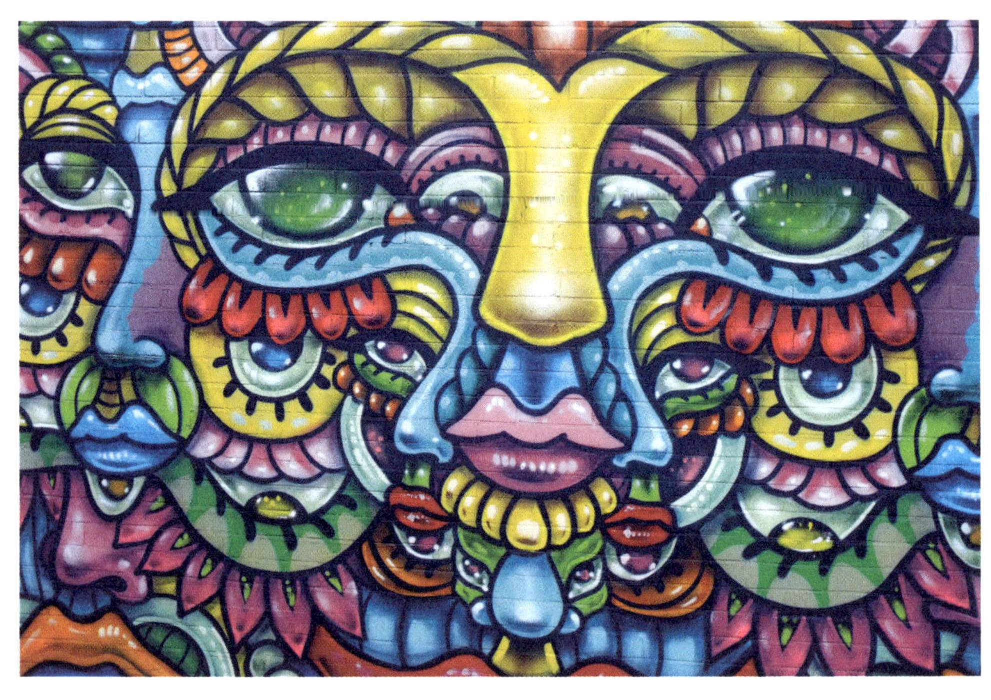

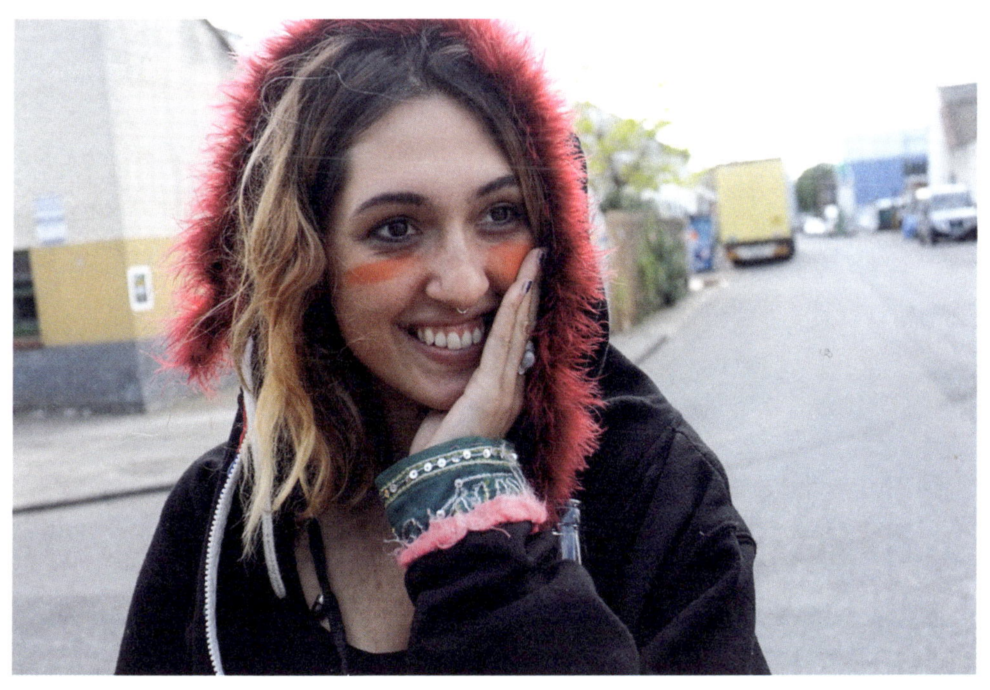

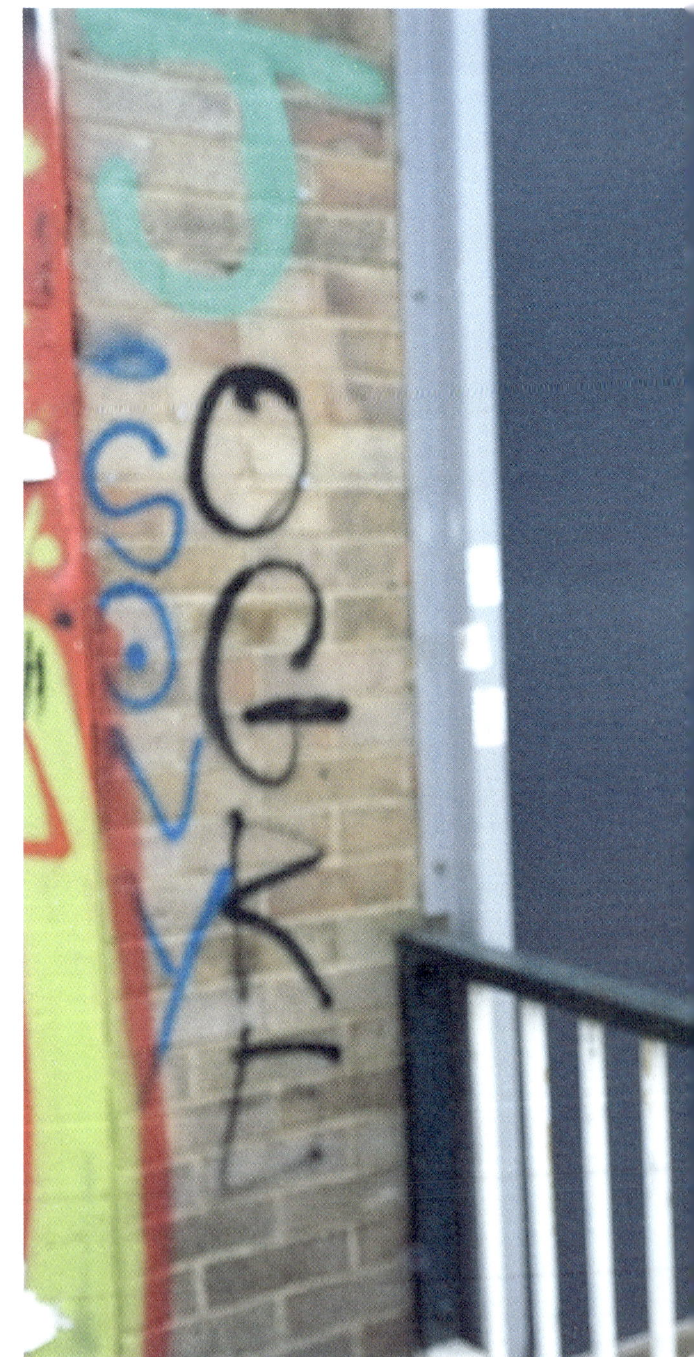

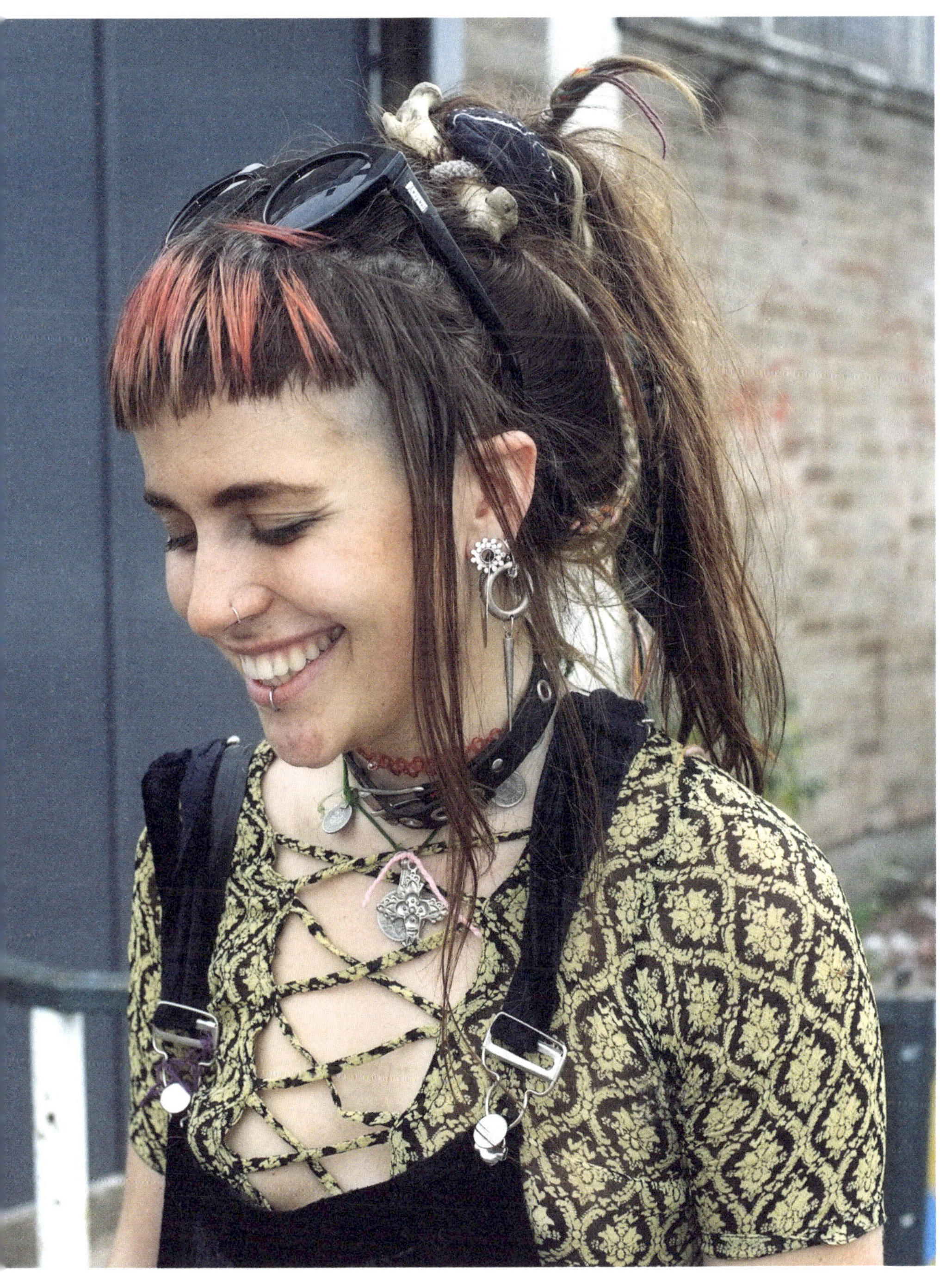

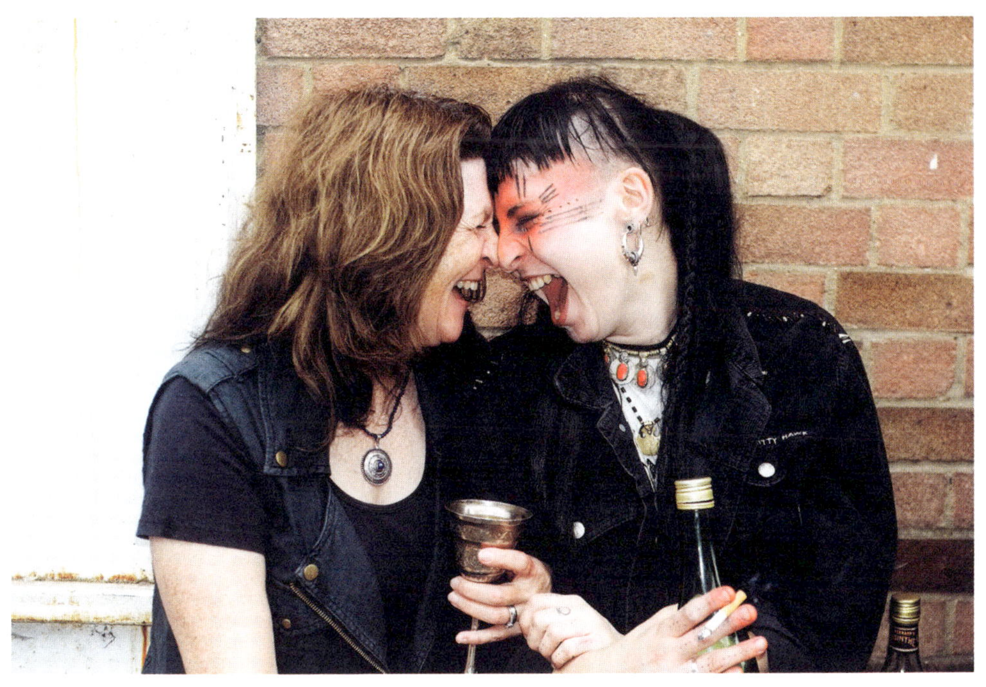

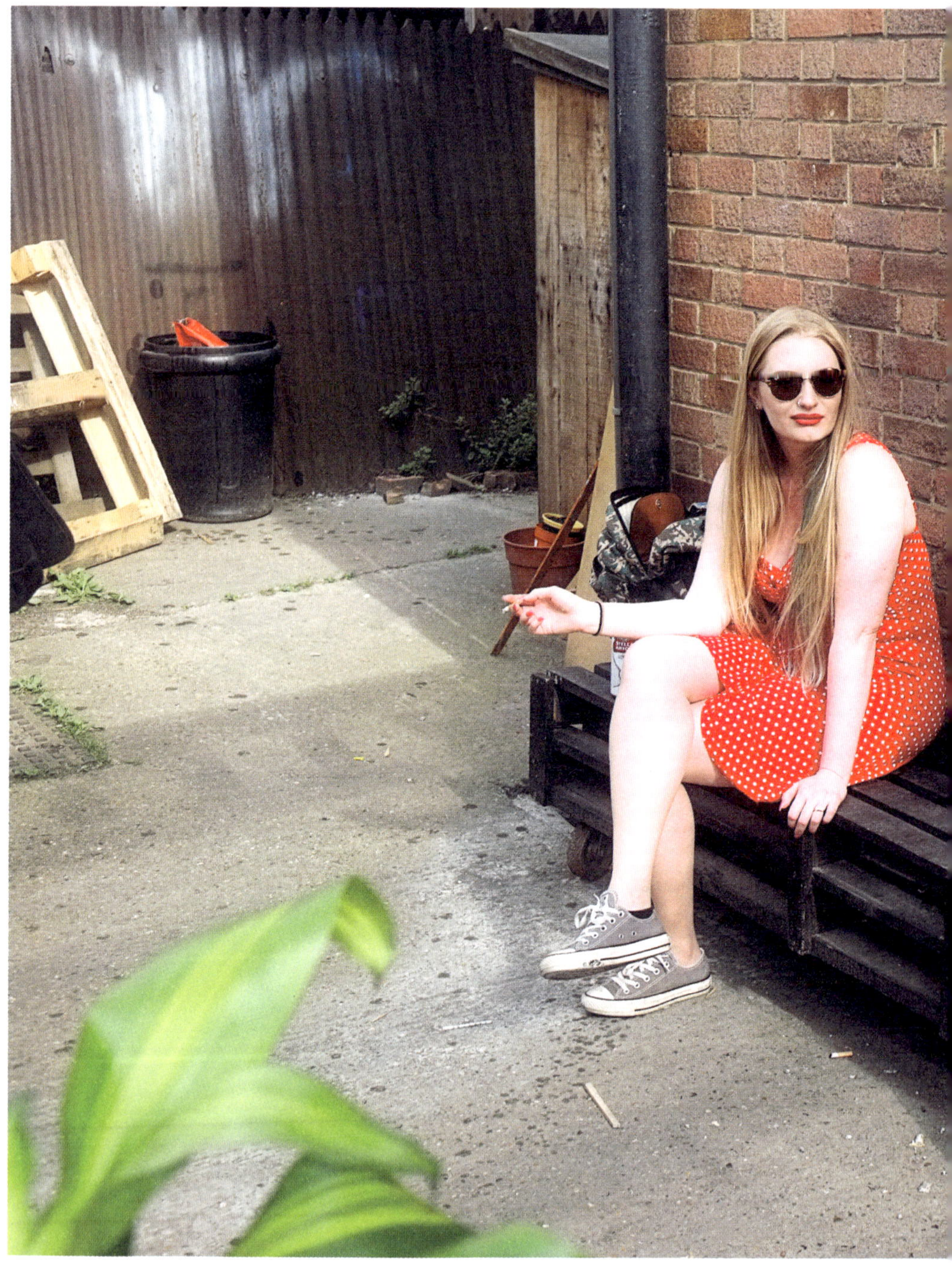

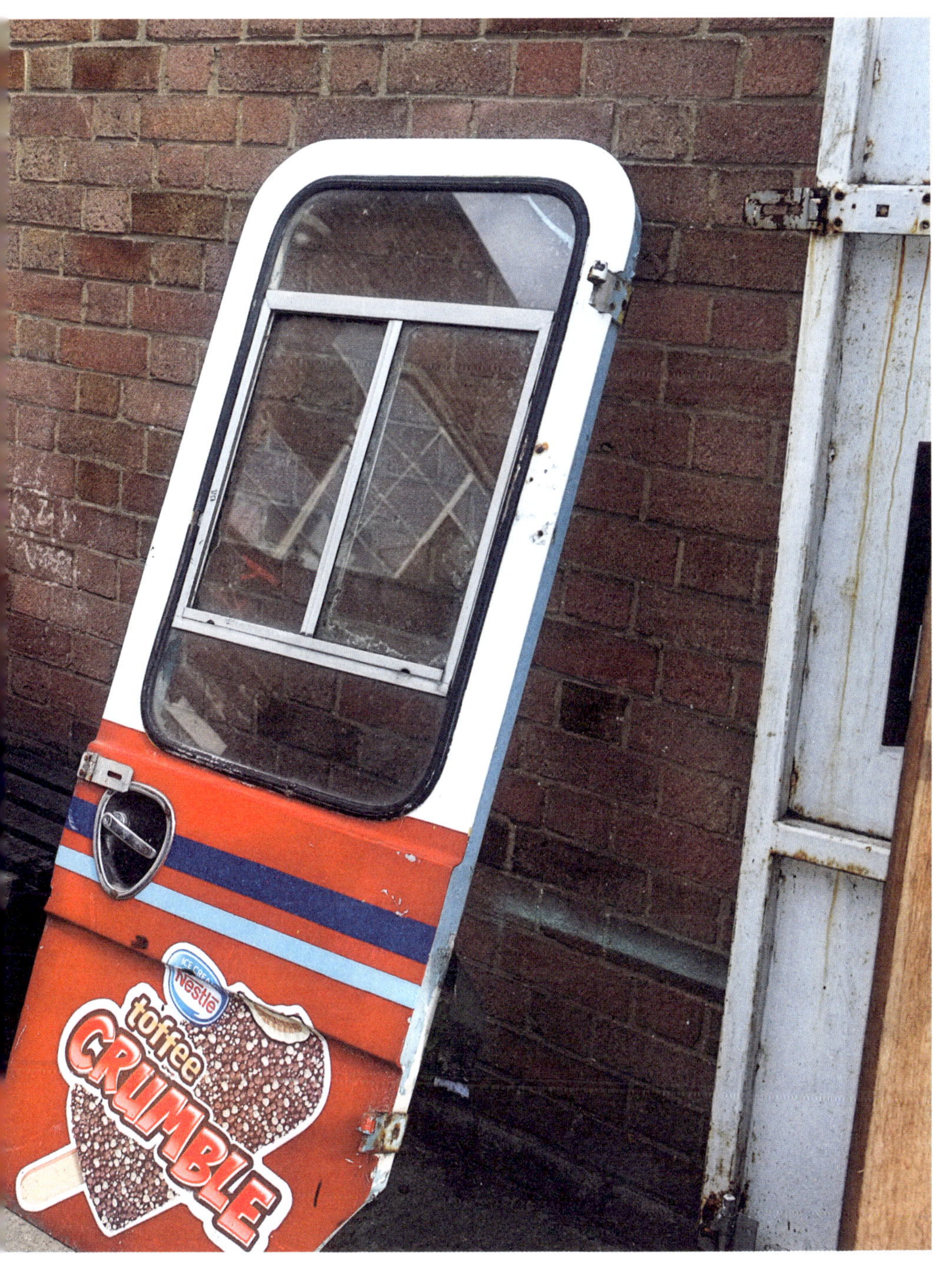
ICE CREAM
Nestlé
toffee
CRUMBLE

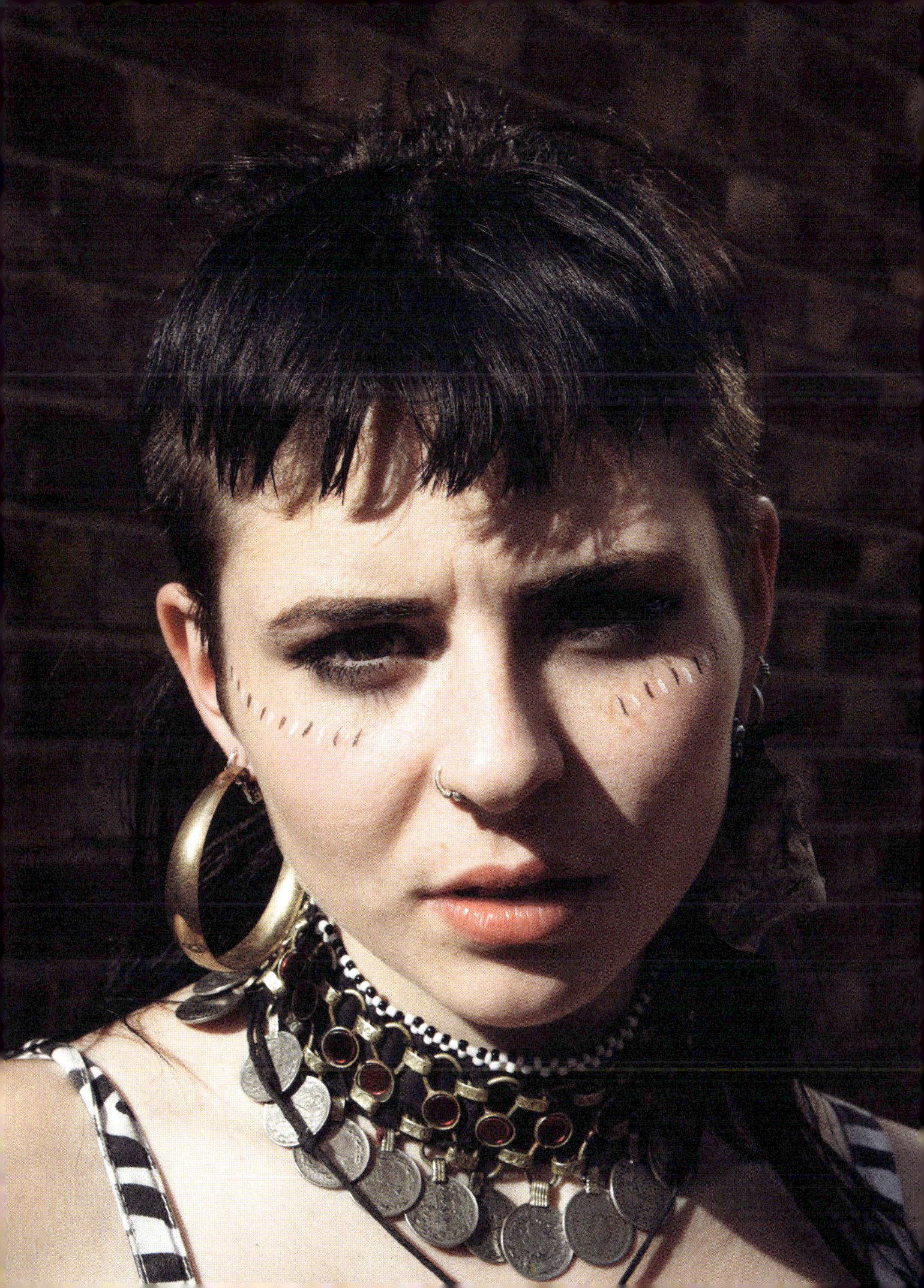

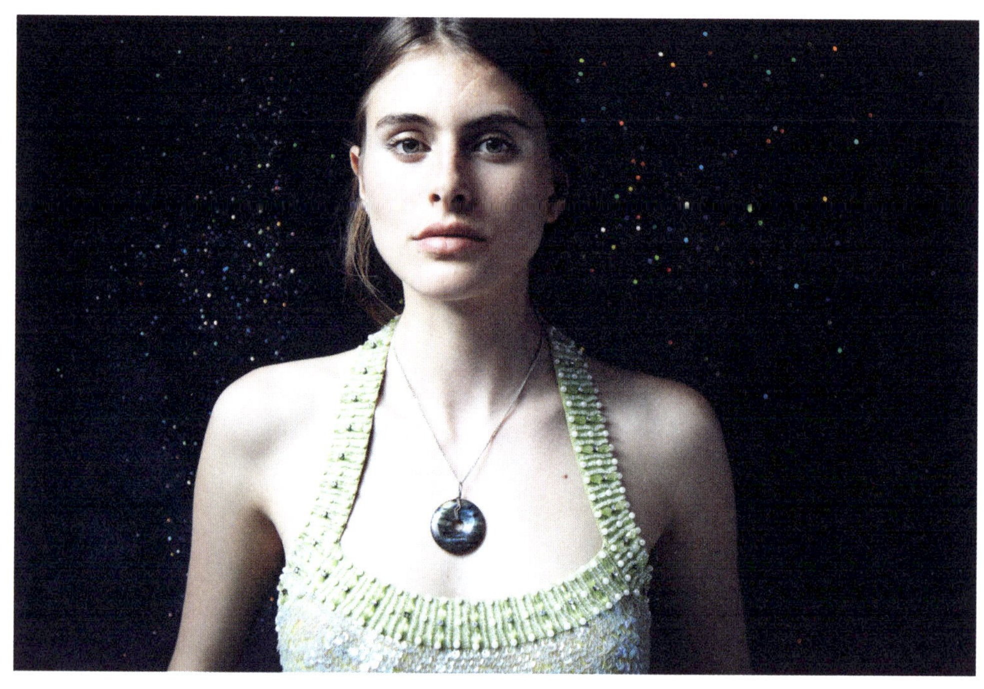

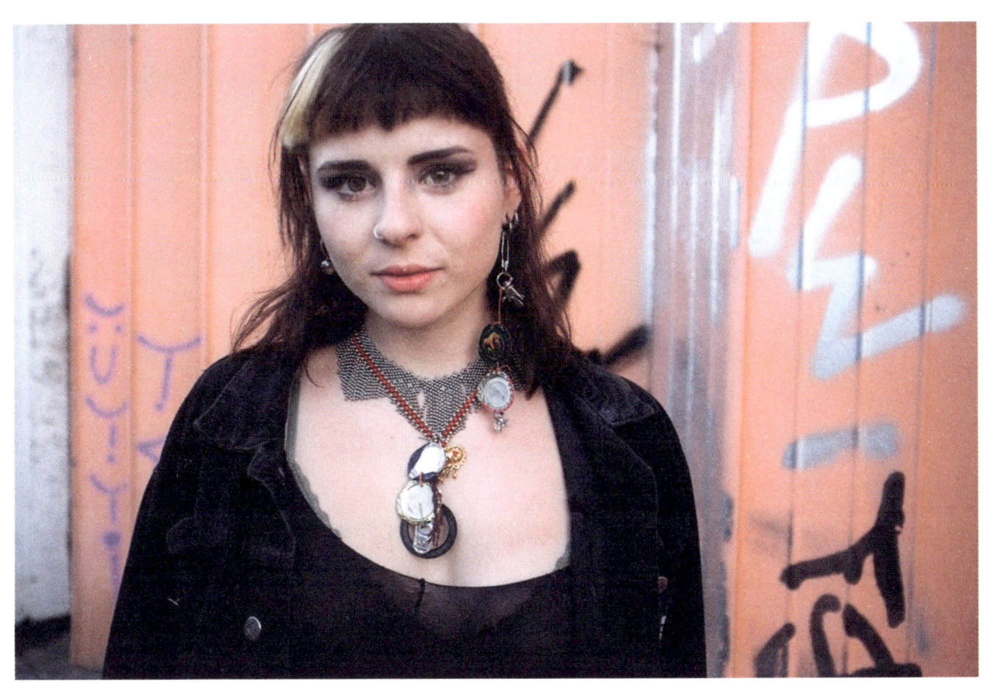

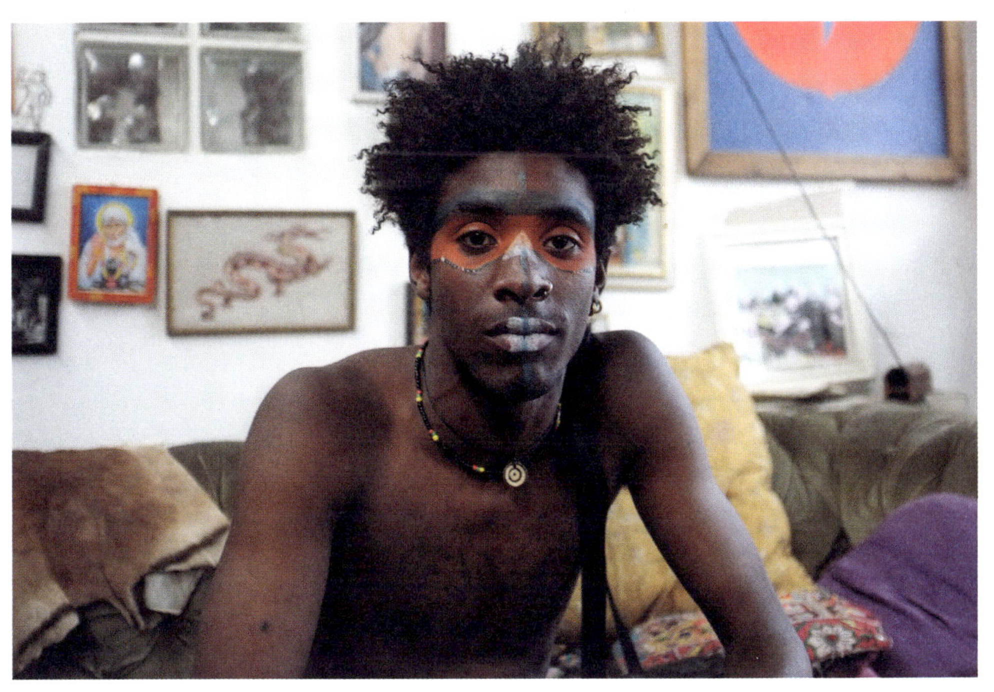

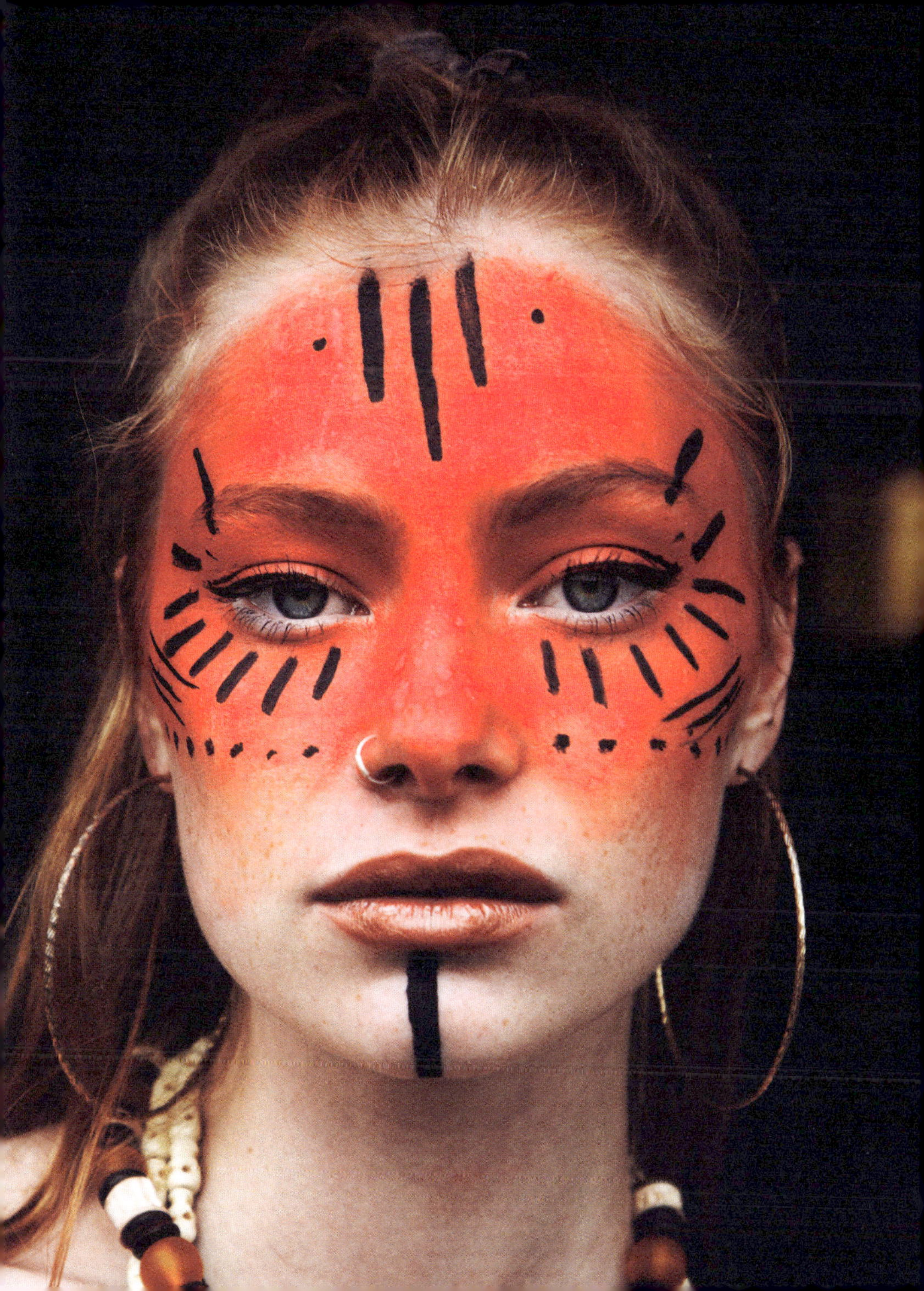

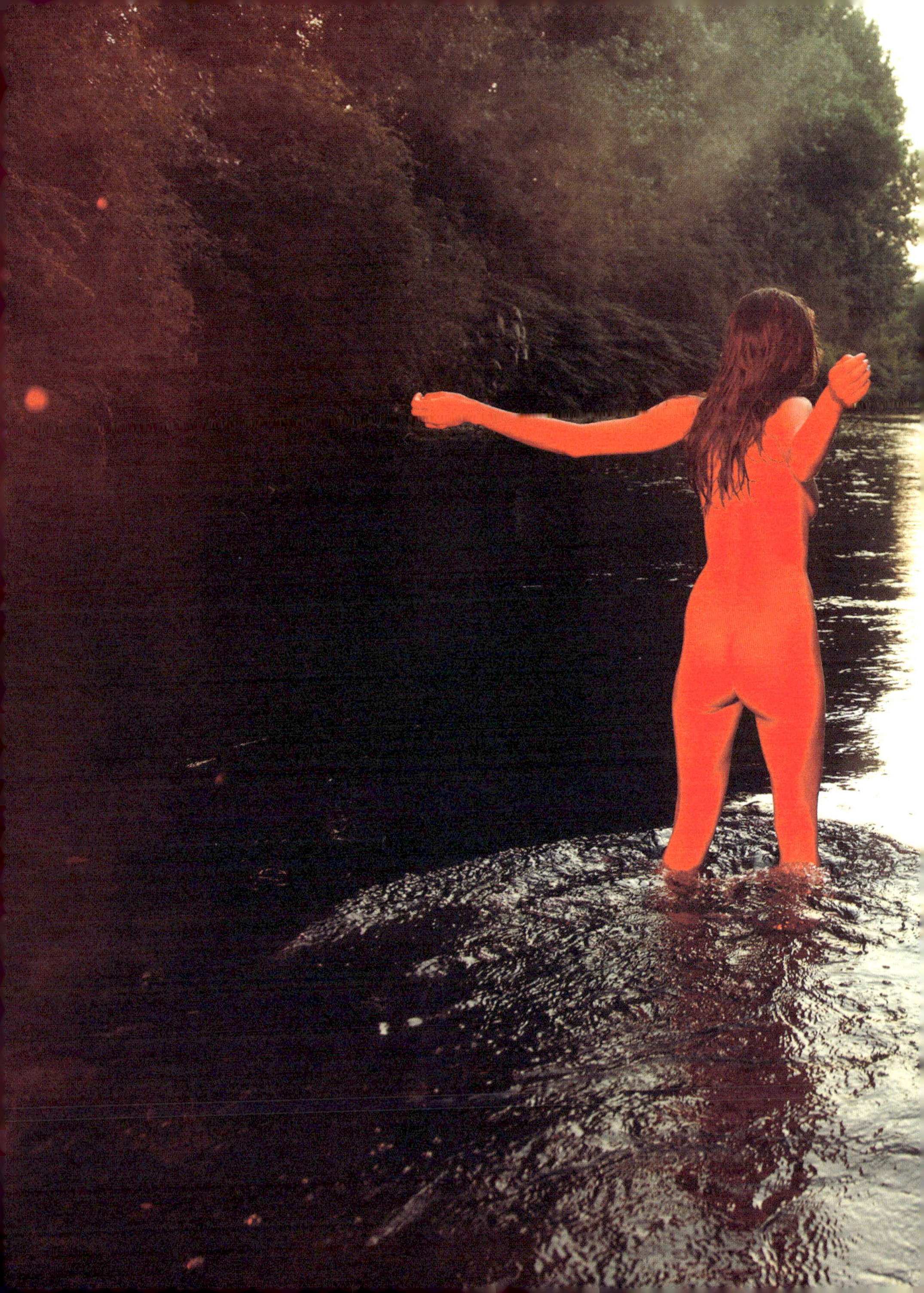

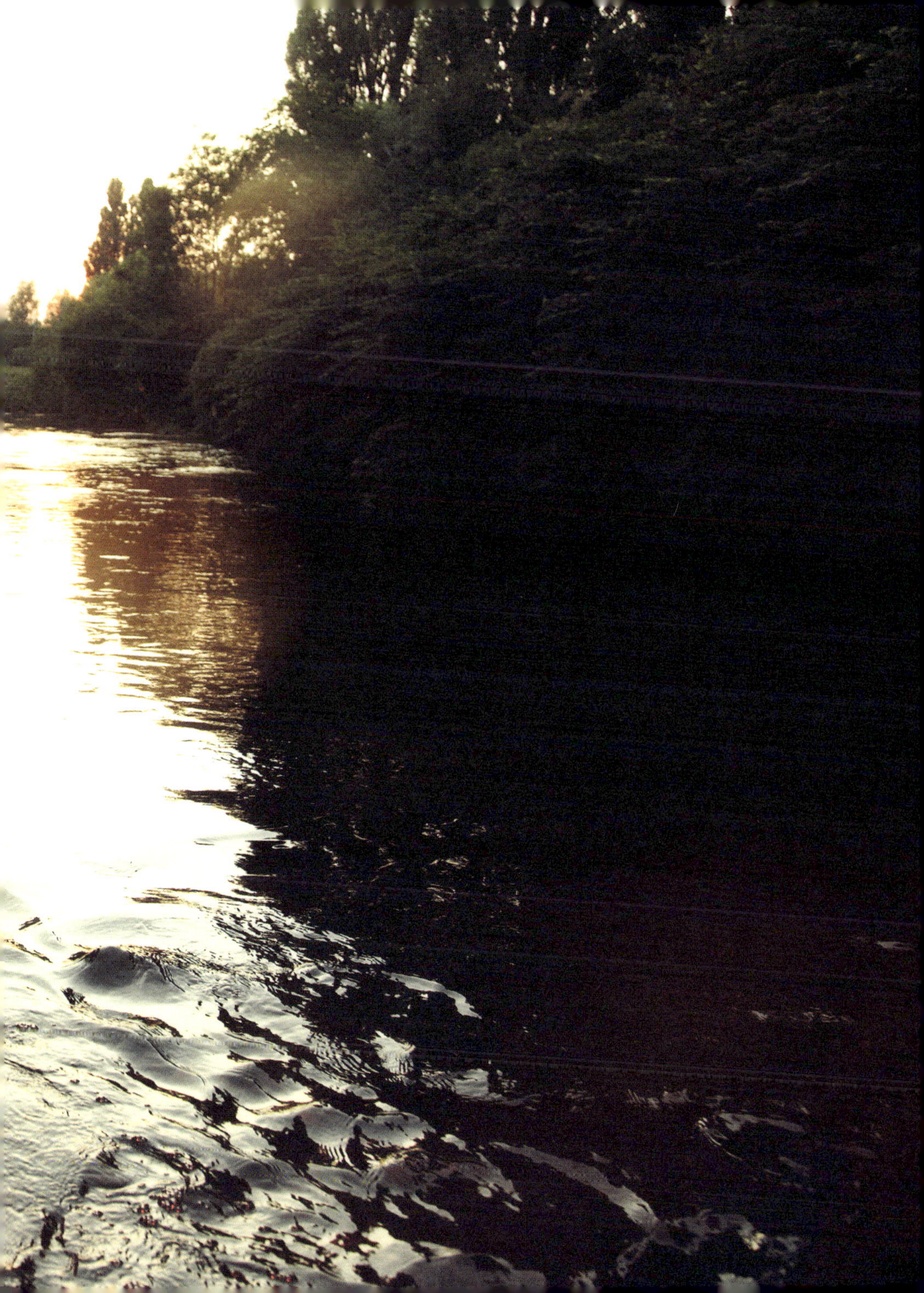

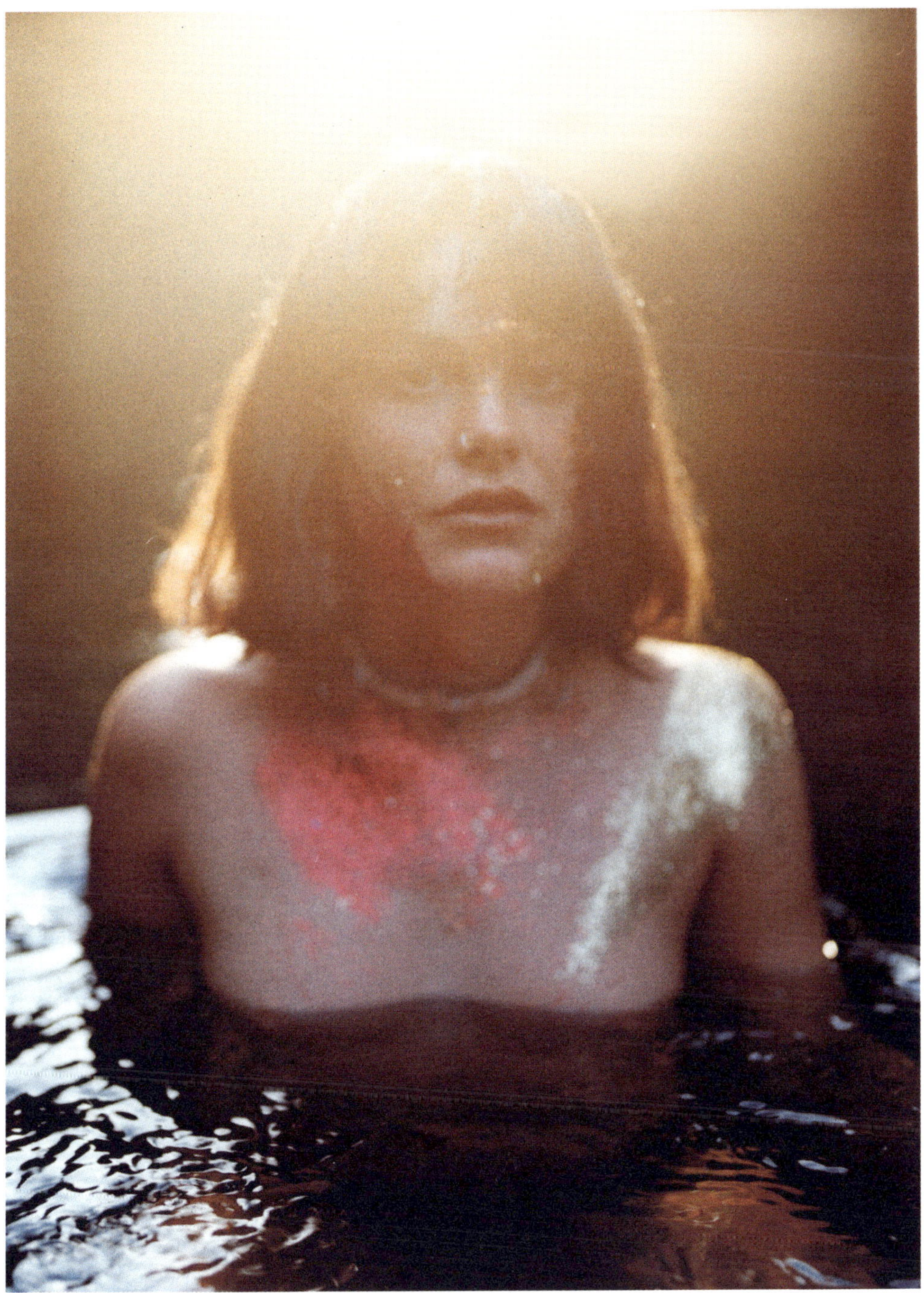

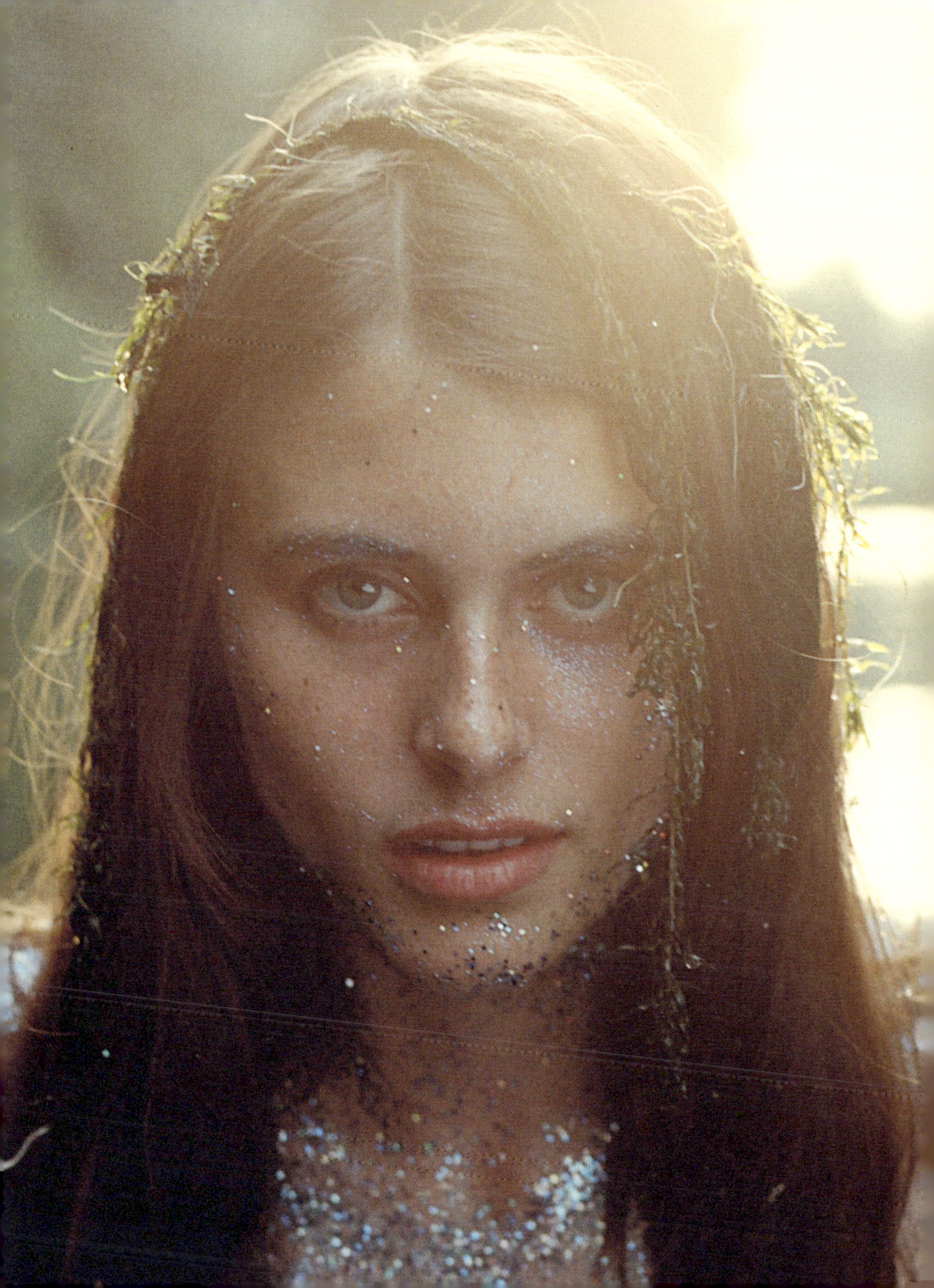

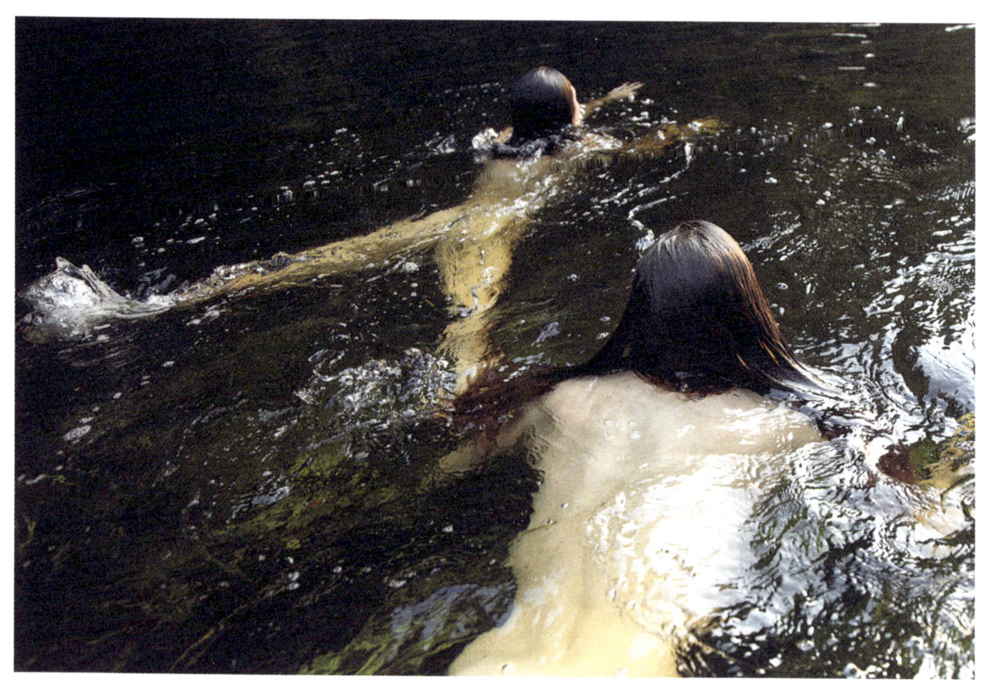

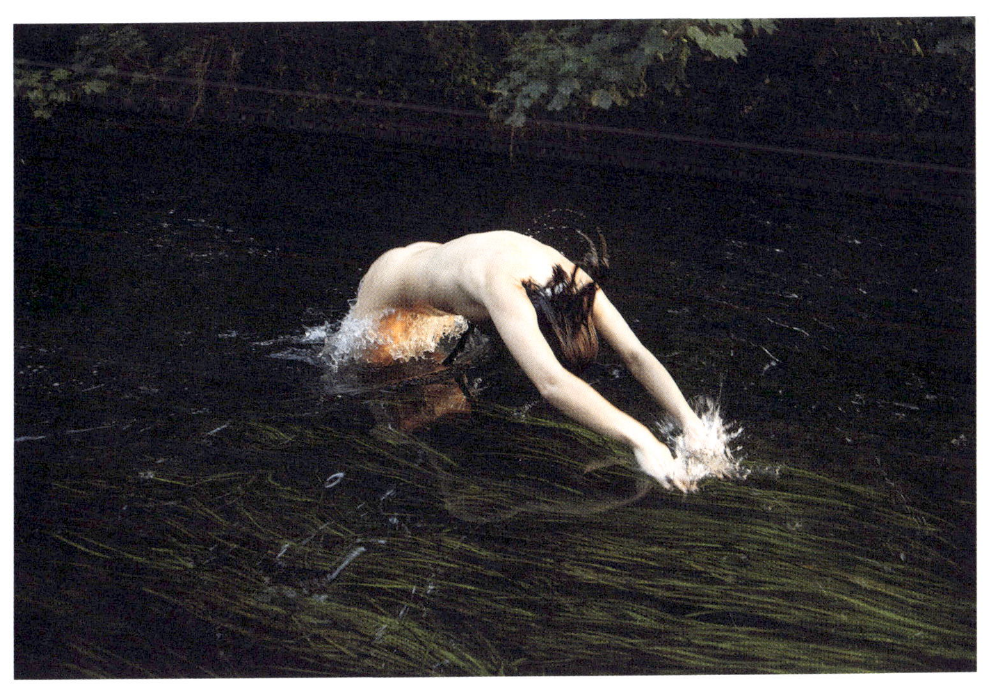

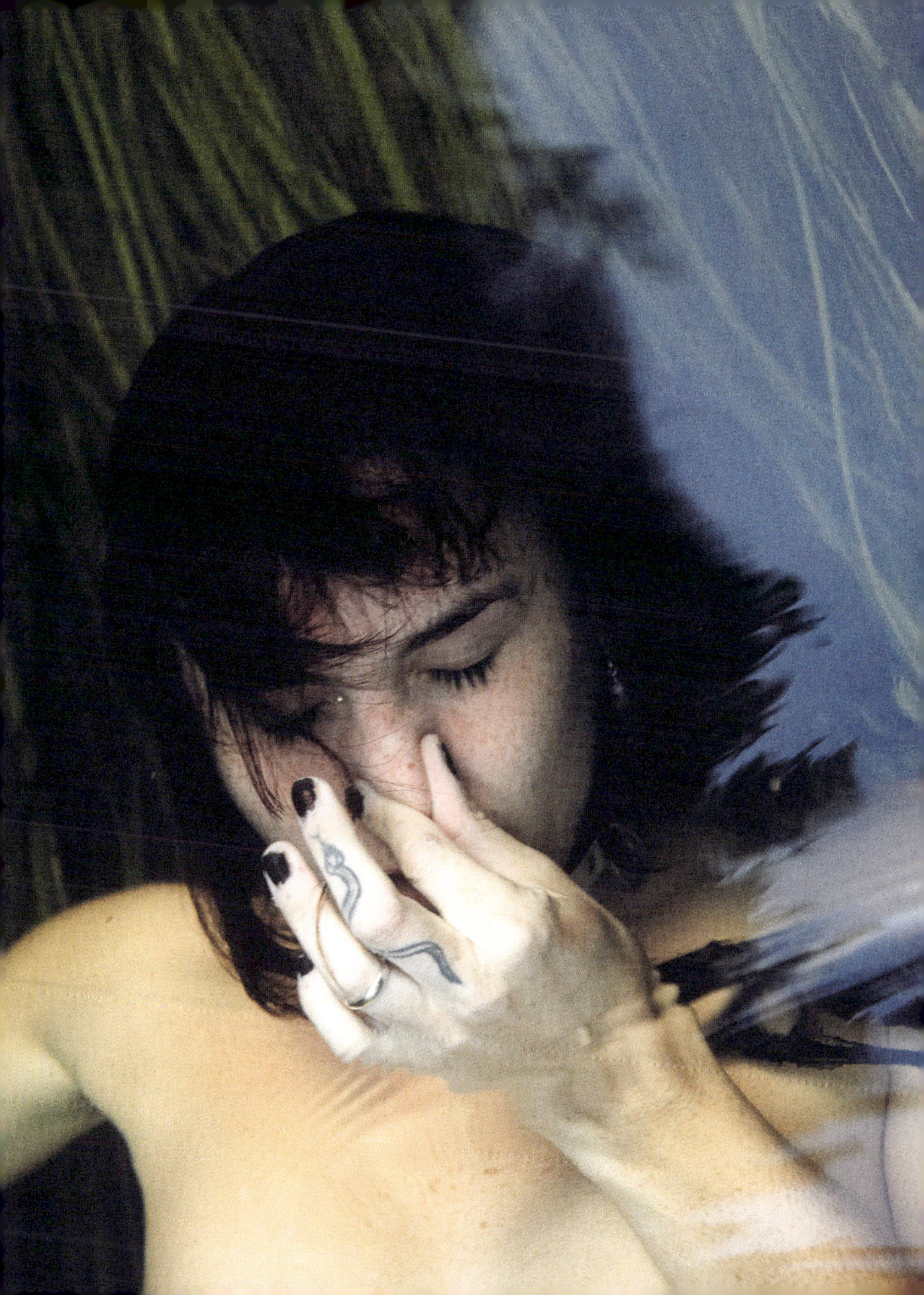

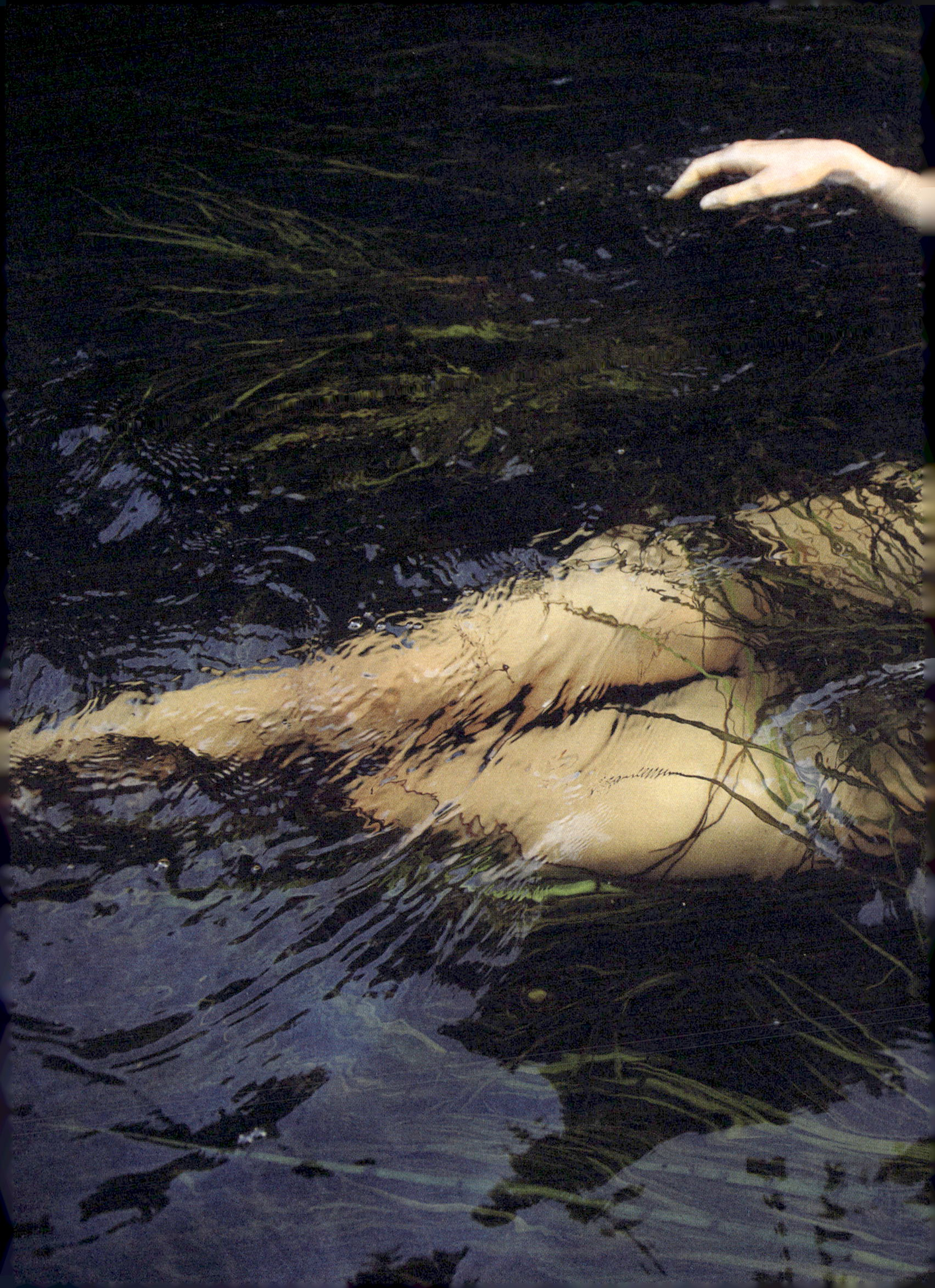

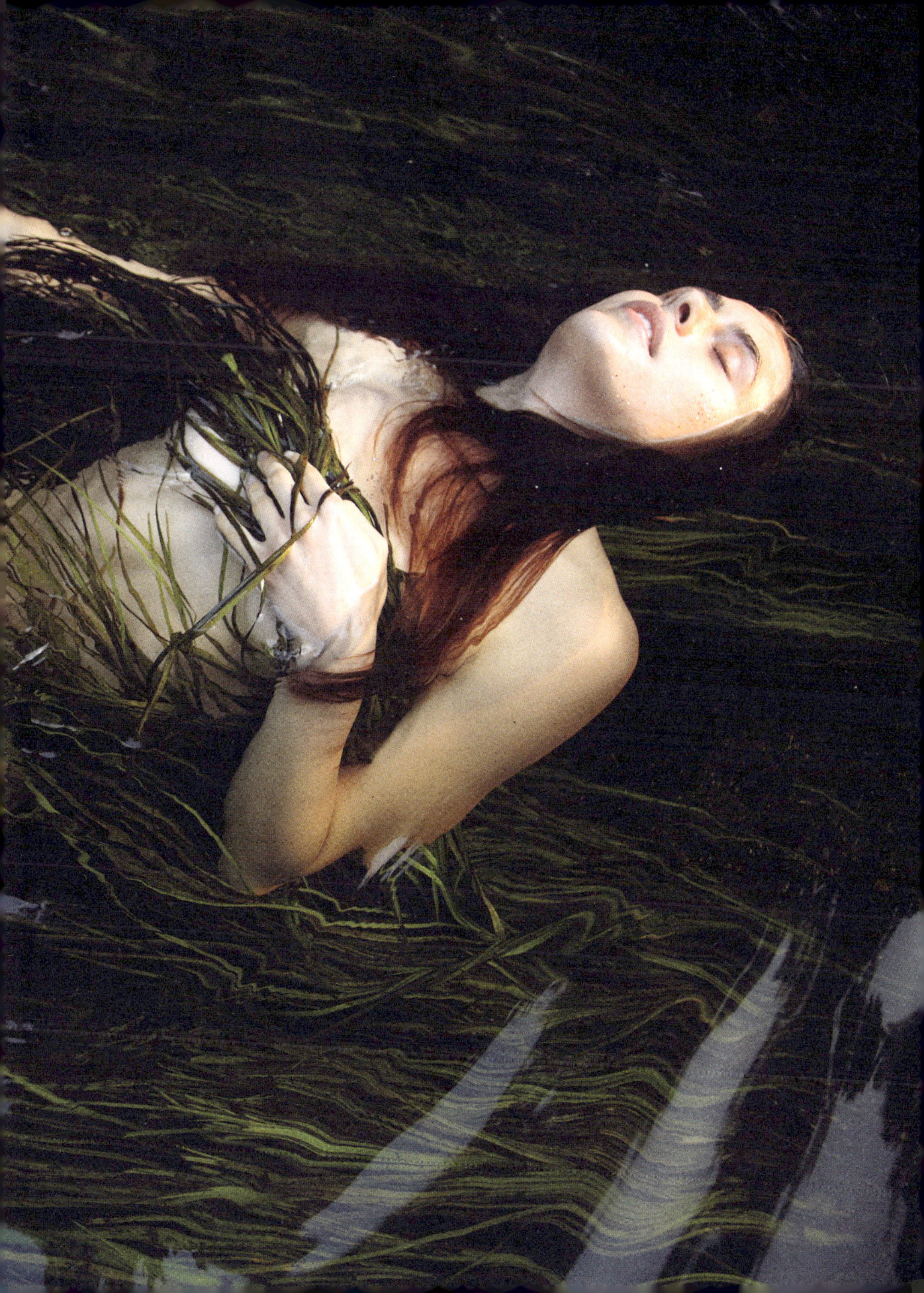

CREDITS

pages 14–21: 'The Re-Psychos' protest costumes by Ellie Walker, performed by the Sisterhood, Tottenham Marsh, 2016

page 28: Ayesha Tan Jones performs as Yaya Bones, Dalston, 2017

page 38: Jemima Nell performs as Binti Red, Tottenham, 2016

page 39: Ayesha Tan Jones performs as Yaya Bones, Tottenham, 2016

pages 47–53: Camilla Mason and Kitty Juby, Camden, 2016

pages 60–67: Muddled Miranda's free party, Epping Forest, 2016

page 66: Totem installation sculptures by Camilla Mason, Tottenham Marsh, 2016

page 67: Charis Bee with forest installations at Muddled Miranda's free party, Epping Forest, 2016

pages 68–71: Ella Lynch wearing her own costumes, Walthamstow, 2016

pages 89–90 and 93: Ayesha Tan Jones at warehouse studio, Manor House, 2017

page 97: Ellie Walker with art installation, Bermondsey, 2016

pages 114–125: Shanti Goupil and Jemima Nell; glitter make-up by Kim Kiefer, River Lea, Hackney Wick, 2017

New Girl Order

First Edition

Copyright © Hoxton Mini Press 2019. All rights reserved.

All photographs © Iain McKell

Introduction text © Gemma Padley

Design and sequence by Friederike Huber, Iain McKell and Hoxton Mini Press

A CIP catalogue record for this book is available from the British Library

ISBN 978-1-910566-48-0

First published in the United Kingdom in 2019 by Hoxton Mini Press

Repro by Touch Digital. Production, design and editorial support from Anna De Pascale, Daniele Roa and Faith McAllister at Hoxton Mini Press.

Printed and bound by Livonia, Latvia

To order books, collector's editions and signed prints please go to:
www.hoxtonminipress.com